FREEDOM AND MAN

FREEDOM AND MAN

A *Wisdom and Discovery Book*

Georgetown University, founded in 1789, observed, under the theme "Wisdom and Discovery for a Dynamic World," its 175th anniversary with a fifteen-month program of lectures, conferences, and symposia on key ideas and issues of our time. From the addresses and deliberations of these events have come the volumes being published as WISDOM AND DISCOVERY BOOKS.

The present volume consists of the papers read at the Patrick F. Healy Conference on Freedom and Man, held on campus on November 30, December 1, and December 2, 1964, and attended by over five thousand persons.

RILEY HUGHES
General Editor

FREEDOM AND MAN

Edited by JOHN COURTNEY MURRAY, S.J.

HANS KÜNG · JOHN COURTNEY MURRAY, S.J.

PIET FRANSEN, S.J. · ROBERT O. JOHANN, S.J.

WILLIAM F. LYNCH, S.J. · DANIEL CALLAHAN

CHRISTOPHER MOONEY, S.J. · JEAN-YVES CALVEZ, S.J.

ERNAN MCMULLIN · CHARLES MALIK

KARL RAHNER, S.J.

A Wisdom and Discovery Book

P. J. KENEDY & SONS · NEW YORK

Nihil obstat: DANIEL V. FLYNN, J.C.D.
            Censor Librorum
Imprimatur: TERENCE J. COOKE, V.G.
            Archdiocese of New York
New York, N. Y., June 23, 1965

CONTENTS

THE CONTRIBUTORS

JOHN COURTNEY MURRAY, S.J., has been professor of dogmatic theology at Woodstock College since 1937 and editor of *Theological Studies* since 1941. He received his B.A. and M.A. from Boston College and his doctorate in theology from the Pontifical Gregorian University, Rome. He was visiting professor of medieval philosophy and culture at Yale University in 1951–1952. Father Murray is a member of the Center for the Study of Democratic Institutions, and serves on the advisory board of the Columbia University Academic Freedom Study. He is the author of *We Hold These Truths: Catholic Reflections on the American Proposition; The Problem of God, Yesterday* and *Today; and The Problem of Religious Freedom*. He is a prominent *peritus* at Vatican Council II.

HANS KÜNG has taught theology at the University of Tübingen since 1960. Born in Switzerland in 1928, and educated there and at the universities of London, Amersterdam, Berlin, and Madrid, he was ordained to the priesthood in 1954. In 1957 he received his doctorate in theology from the Institut Catholique, Paris. Father Küng is co-editor of *Tübinger Theologische Quartalscrift*. Among his books translated into English and published in this country are *The Doctrine of Karl Barth, with a Catholic Reflection; The Council, Reform and Reunion;* and *That the World May Believe*.

PIET FRANSEN, S.J., a Belgian by birth, holds the chair of philosophy at the University of Innsbruck, succeeding Karl Rahner. He previously taught in the Jesuit Faculty of Theology at Louvain. In this country, he has taught at Fordham University. Father Fransen has written extensively about Vatican Council II; he addressed several groups of bishops on the question of Grace during the Council's second session. A contributor to many periodicals in Europe and the United States, he is the author of *Divine Grace and Man* and *Faith and the Sacraments*.

WILLIAM F. LYNCH, S.J., is currently writer in residence at St. Peter's College, Jersey City, N. J. He holds a Ph.D. in classics from Fordham University. He directed classical theater productions at Fordham and was editor of *Thought* for many years. From 1959 to 1962 he was visiting professor of English at Georgetown University

7

and consultant to the Honors Program of its College of Arts and Sciences. Father Lynch is the author of *The Image Industries; Christ and Apollo: The Dimension of the Literary Imagination; The Integrating Mind: An Exploration into Western Thought;* and *An Approach to the Metaphysics of Plato through the Parmenides.* With Walter J. Burghardt, S.J., he edited *The Idea of Catholicism.*

CHRISTOPHER F. MOONEY, S.J., is assistant professor of theology at Fordham University and director of the American Institute of Spirituality. He received his B.A. and M.A. at Loyola University (Chicago) and his doctorate at the Institut Catholique, Paris. He entered the Society of Jesus in 1944 and was ordained a priest in 1957. He has contributed articles to *Thought, Theological Studies, Harvard Theological Review, Downside Review,* and *Scripture.* His book *Teilhard de Chardin and the Mystery of Christ* will shortly appear in French and English.

ERNAN McMULLIN is currently visiting lecturer in the philosophy of science at the University of Minnesota. Born in Donegal, Ireland, Father McMullin received the B.Sc. and B.D. degrees from Maynooth College and the Ph.D. from Louvain. He has been a member of the department of philosophy at the University of Notre Dame since 1954. Father McMullin is editor of *The Concept of Matter* and of the forthcoming *Galileo Galilei.* He has contributed articles to *New Scholasticism, Modern Schoolman, Irish Theological Quarterly, Revue Philosophique de Louvain,* and other periodicals. He is president of the American Catholic Philosophical Association.

ROBERT O. JOHANN, S.J., is associate professor of philosophy and adjunct professor of Christian ethics at Fordham University. He was visiting associate professor of philosophy at Yale University for 1963–1964. He has been a Councillor of the Metaphysical Society of America since 1962. A graduate of St. Louis University, he holds an S.T.L. from Woodstock College and a Ph.D. from Louvain. He is the author of *The Meaning of Love,* and a contributor to *Experience, Existence, and the Good,* edited by I. C. Lieb, and to *The Concept of Matter,* edited by Ernan McMullin. His articles have appeared in *Cross Currents, Review of Metaphysics, Thought,* and other journals.

DANIEL CALLAHAN is an associate editor of *The Commonweal.* A graduate of Yale, he took his M.A. at Georgetown and studied for his doctorate at Harvard. He has taught in the departments of religion of the Harvard Divinity School and of Temple and Brown universities. A contributor on current questions to many periodicals, he is the author of *The Mind of the Catholic Layman* and *Honesty in the Church*. He is the editor of *Generation of the Third Eye: Young Catholic Leaders View Their Church* and *Federal Aid to Catholic Schools*.

JEAN-YVES CALVEZ, S.J., is assistant director of Action Populaire, a social institute conducted by the Jesuits at Vanves, France. A consultant on the document on the Church and the modern world to Vatican Council II, he has lectured widely in Japan and the United States and has studied social institutions throughout Africa and Latin America. He is the author of *The Church and Social Justice* and *The Social Thought of John XXIII*. His major work *La Pensée de Karl Marx* is shortly to appear in an English translation.

CHARLES MALIK, philosopher, educator, and statesman, was born in Lebanon in 1906. After graduating from the American University of Beirut, he took his M.A. and Ph.D. at Harvard. He taught philosophy at the American University of Beirut from 1937 to 1956, serving as dean of graduate studies in 1955–1956. He was Minister of Lebanon to the United States from 1945 to 1953 and Ambassador from 1953 to 1955. A member of the Lebanon delegation to the UN from 1945 to 1958, he was President of the 13th Session of the UN General Assembly. He is the author of *War and Peace, The Problem of Asia, The Problem of Coexistence, Christ and Crisis*, and *Man in the Struggle for Peace*.

KARL RAHNER, S.J., an officially appointed theologian to Vatican Council II, is professor of dogmatic theology at the University of Innsbruck. Born in Freiburg, Germany, in 1904, he studied philosophy and theology at the universities of Munich, Freiburg, Innsbruck, and Valkenburg (Netherlands), and worked for two years under Martin Heidegger. Father Rahner is the author of nearly eight hundred articles on theological, philosophical, and religious subjects. He is the editor of *The Dictionary of Theology* and of the multi-volume encyclopedia *Sacramentum Mundi*. Among his many books are *Inquiries, Nature and Grace, Dilemmas in the Modern Church, On the Theology of Death*, and *The Dynamic Element in the Church*.

Foreword

John Courtney Murray, S.J.

None of the speakers at the Patrick F. Healy Conference on Freedom and Man is likely to forget the occasion or the audience. The audience itself may forget, as audiences do, what the speakers said. Therefore this volume will be a useful reminder. In any case, I hope that the audience will not forget what brought it together. It is a striking event when more than five thousand people converge upon a university for three days to listen, with an alertness that was palpable in the atmosphere, to a series of discourses, none of which (save perhaps my own) were in the popular vein, so called. Only the theme itself can give the clue to the significance of the event and to the reason for the throng.

It may be that the word "freedom" has lost some of the political magic that it had in the nineteenth century. But this is only because the simplicities of the Political Century are no longer available to us in an age in which the fact and the theme of "socialization" also claim attention. Freedom, of course, continues to be what Lord Acton said it was, the highest political end. Today, however, we have come to understand better the complex conditions of its attainment. Freedom as a political end, or even as the political method, recedes beyond realization in a society which fails to reckon with the full truth about man and with all the exigencies of the order of justice among men. In particular, the noble phrase, the "free society," can have no more than a merely formalistic meaning, if love be lacking among the citizenry, if hatreds rend the body politic. Today political discourse about freedom must have more solid substance, if it is to be taken

11

seriously by the peoples of the world whose personal and corporate lives feel increasingly the impact of Teilhard de Chardin's law of complexification.

The audience at Georgetown did not lack interest in freedom as a political and social problem. And the theme of the Conference itself required that this interest be met. The man whose freedom was under discussion is forever political and social man. Hence the discussion did not neglect these aspects of the problem. I think, however, that the chief interest of the audience had another focus. I shall not hesitate to call it theological. The audience was most evidently aware, as were all the speakers, that the Church is entering the Age of Renewal. The full profile of the new age has not yet emerged into clear definition. One feature, however, already stands out. Freedom is the feature. It is visible on the face that Vatican Council II has presented to a watching world. It will also be marked on the face of the new historical epoch into which the Council is moving a world that awaits the movement.

Some have greeted the new age with gladness; others, who are fewer, view it with alarm. Both reactions are superficial. The problem is to understand what it may legitimately mean to say that a new age of Christian freedom begins to dawn. It was, I think, the desire to make this effort at understanding that formed the common bond among the five thousand people who came to listen to men who were themselves engaged in the same effort. This was my reason for saying that I hoped the audience would not forget what brought it together. For the effort will be long, and it must be sustained. It must be sustained as it was begun, by searching study and by continued conversation.

The essays that follow deal with a wide variety of topics. They exhibit, however, a certain unity in that all of them develop in one way or another the theme of Christian freedom. (It need hardly be said, though it should be said, that to qualify freedom as Christian is not to impart to the word any sort of sectarian sense. Like the grace of Christ, the freedom that is Christian is given outside the confines of the visible Church.) The theme is fundamental. In the Prologue to his lengthy treatise on man and the moral life, St. Thomas states the unique human prerogative that is also the indispensable condition of all religion and morality. Man, he says, "is made in the image of God; and by image here is meant that man is intelligent, free in his power of choice, and of himself the master of himself . . . the active source of what he does." The statement contains an implicit citation from St. John Damascene which sums up the Greek patristic exegesis of the first thing said about man in the Scriptures (Gen. 1:26–27).

Father Rahner, as is his wont, pursues this truth about man into the depths of its mystery. It is not that man has the power to choose this or that, now and again. To say that man is free is to say that he can, and in the end will, make the final and definitive choice that is fraught with eternal consequence. Man can choose God or choose to reject God. Freedom is mystery indeed. Moreover, to say that man is free is also to say, with Teilhard de Chardin (and with his gifted interpreter in this volume, Father Mooney), that man faces the risk of the cosmic *hamartia*—a refusal, a failure, a falling short that would defeat the intention of evolution, which is man's personal ascent to the higher consciousness and his corporate growth into a community of love.

As the first truth about man is that he is free, so the first truth about Christ is that He is Liberator, the One through whom man is set free. St. Paul, speaking in the name of humanity, cried out for deliverance from "this body of death" (Rom. 7:24) which is the human environment, external and internal. And he proclaimed the good news that deliverance is at hand: "For the law of the Spirit of life in Christ Jesus has set me free from the law of sin and death" (8:2). This is Father Fransen's general theme. Man's liberation, moreover, is a rescue from isolation and from all its possibilities of errancy. It is a gathering into the Church, under her governance and guidance. Therefore the experience of the freedom for which Christ has set us free (cf. Gal. 5:1) is an experience of the polar tension between freedom and authority. The Christian experiences his freedom as also duty, as obedience, as responsibility, as being-for-the-others in community. This is the experience, often sacrificial, with which Father Johann, Mr. Callahan and Professor Küng deal, in different ways and from different standpoints.

Father Lynch points out the way to Christian freedom. It hardly seems, on a superficial view, to be a royal way, since it leads through all the density of the human, all the limitations of the finite, all the contingency of the historical moment, whose demands are ever unique, to be met by personal judgment and choice. But there is no other way. It is man who is free, and only free to be free humanly, not magically, within the full reality of the human, whose basic law has been defined: "Only that ought not to be which cannot be." In his turn, Professor McMullin selects a particular topic—freedom and the progress of science— out of the general theme that freedom is the principle of man's development in human living, the dynamism of his movement toward his own perfection. I myself, in taking up the subject of religious freedom, touch on one sector of the larger problem of preserving about the human person in society a certain zone or sphere of freedom, within which man must be immune from coercive constraints and restraints in the pursuit of the highest values of the person as such, who transcends society in virtue of his direct relatedness to the truth and to God who is the Truth. In what concerns religion, the dignity of man requires that he decide and act on the bidding or forbidding of his own conscience. No human agency may bring force to bear on him in restraint of his free exercise of religion according to conscience, unless and until it is proved in the case that his action offends against the legitimate requirements of public order. Finally, this same problem of the personal and corporate freedom of man in society is further pursued by Father Calvez in all the complexity that it presents within the conditions of our technological age.

Thus discourse on freedom leads one into all the areas of human thought, concern, and action. These essays show that the problem is never simple and easily solved. Within the Church the issue has a special delicacy and difficulty. Unless this is well understood, there will be no Age of Renewal, only an age of change, to be followed inevitably by retrogression. Freedom is indeed the first truth about man. But if the truth be debased, it becomes man's most destructive illusion. "Live as free men," St. Peter exhorts the faithful, "yet without using your freedom as a pretext for evil, but live as servants of God" (1 Peter 2:16). "It was unto freedom that you were called," St. Paul proclaims, but he too adds the warning, "only do not use your freedom as an opportunity for the flesh, but through love be servants of one another" (Gal. 5:13). The injunction, following the warning, says the final inexhaustible word about Christian freedom. Freedom, say philosophers today, is man's very existence. They are not wrong, within the limits of philosophy. But Paul suggests the higher truth. Freedom is love. It is the experience of the new law whereby the children of God live.

It is both fitting and necessary, in conclusion, to express the gratitude of Georgetown University, and my own, to Father George H. Dunne, S.J., Director of the 175th Anniversary program, who conceived, planned, and organized the Conference, and to Professor Riley Hughes for the unwearied cheerfulness and most exact care with which he carried through the laborious task of assembling these essays and preparing them for publication.

Woodstock College
May 24, 1965

GOD'S FREE SPIRIT IN THE CHURCH *

HANS KÜNG

With all its failures, the Second Vatican Council has achieved a powerful breakthrough toward a new freedom in the Catholic Church. All mankind became joyfully aware of this new freedom, candor, and adaptability shown by the Catholic Church in our time. Nevertheless, some well-meaning members of our Church— and I think we should understand their concern—felt a certain anxiety, even some fear, when faced with this new freedom, candor, and adaptability. Would not the Church, which hitherto has proven itself a stable column and foundation of truth, also be drawn into the ruinous instability and evanescence of all earthly things? What, then, is to become of the truth which the Church has always proclaimed? And how are we to regard the *Spirit* of truth who has always taught the Church all truth? Why should everything suddenly be changed?

God's Spirit Is a Free Spirit

Clearly, one can understand the Church only if he understands the Spirit that moves the Church, moves it really and ultimately. Of course many spirits move the Church: good ones and bad ones— human spirits. Yet according to the belief of the Catholic Church and Christianity (in this Church, but also in the other Christian

* Because of a conflict in copyright, Father Küng's original paper is unavailable for this volume; he presents here his most recent reflections on the subject of freedom in the Church.

17

churches), above all human spirits there is another whose power is altogether different, a mysterious, free Spirit: the Holy Spirit.

It would be dangerous to identify the Holy Spirit with the Church: the Holy Spirit is not the Church, but the Spirit of God. On that truth is based the fundamental *freedom* of the Holy Spirit. Just as the Holy Spirit is never simply the spirit of the Christian, so he is never the spirit of the Church. He is the Spirit of God. Nowhere in the New Testament is the Holy Spirit called "Spirit of the Church," but always either "Spirit of God," or "Spirit of Jesus Christ." This Spirit emerges neither from the Church nor from the Christian, but only from God himself. He is not the bestowal and gift, the power and strength of the Church, but of God. He acts *on* the Church, manifests himself *to* the Church, comes *to* the Church, establishes and maintains the Church. But he does not become the Church's own spirit. He remains God's own Spirit. Therefore he is and remains the *free* Spirit.

We are the Church, we human beings, we the community of men believing in Christ. We are the Church—a human structure. But the Holy Spirit is not something created by man; he is the Divine Spirit. There is no identity, but a fundamental difference, between the Divine Spirit and the Church created by man. Yet this difference is not only generally, in an abstract sense, the ontological difference between the divine and the human. We speak, after all, of an actual Church. And this actual Church is not only a Church consisting of men, but of sinful men. This real Church is not only a human Church, but at the same time a sinful Church. For we are the Church: we, completely forgiven and yet again sinful men, we, the community of men absolved yet always newly dependent upon remission: *communio sanctorum*, to be sure, but also, and unfortunately, *communio peccatorum*. We the Church are an erring creation. The Spirit of God, however, is not sinful, but on the contrary, the holy, thoroughly holy Spirit. Therefore we see once more, and in a considerably more profound sense, that he is the free Spirit, the Spirit truly free from sin, fault, and death.

From this free Divine Spirit we derive our understanding of the Church and of ourselves. But the free Spirit of God must not simply be thought of as part of the Church. In order to avoid a confusion of Spirit and Church, it is better not to speak of the Church as a "godly-human," or even "divine" institution. Surely the individual believer does not become a "godly-human" or even "divine" being because he is possessed by the Spirit. Again, to avoid confounding Spirit and Church, it is better not to speak of an organic development and expansion of the Church and its Spirit. (The romantic-idealistic concept of ecclesiastical history disregards the fundamental difference between the perfect Divine Spirit and the Church. Owing to the disparity between Spirit and Church, the Church often develops erroneously or retrogresses.) Finally, in order to avoid confusion of Spirit and Church, it is also better not to speak of the "sense of faith of the Church" (*sensus fidelium*) as of a revelation of the Holy Spirit. The sense of faith of the Church can never become source and norm for the revelation of the Holy Spirit. On the contrary, the revelation of the Spirit always is and remains the source and norm for the *sensus fidelium* of the Church. Here it is shown very concretely that the Holy Spirit in the Church is and remains a free Spirit.

The importance of seeing the difference between the Spirit and the Church is apparent. Only in this light can the human, all-too-human, behavior, the lapses and shortcomings, the sins and faults, of the Church be taken seriously and in the full, liberating manner. After all, a Church which identifies itself with the Holy Spirit cannot say a *confiteor*. It cannot and must not admit that it has failed in thought, word, and deed, greatly failed through its own fault, through its grievous fault. Instead it is forced, time and again, to feeble theological subterfuges and to apologetics that convince no one. In short, it must succumb to an idealistic, triumphalistic, and deluded conception of itself. It cannot, therefore, be a *free* Church.

Only if it is free can the Church truly and in freedom listen to the Holy Spirit and obey him. For a Church which identifies itself with the Holy Spirit does not need, after all, to listen, to believe, to obey any longer. It knows everything already, it does everything already. All it needs is to listen to itself, to obey itself, to believe in itself, and to enjoin the *others* outside the Church to listen, believe, and obey. Finally, it must succumb to an autocratic, egocentric conception of itself. Again, it will not be a *free* Church.

A Church, on the other hand, which recognizes the distinction between the Holy Spirit and the Church may thus take seriously the sinning and failing of the Church: realistically, humbly, but also in the consoling hope of a new redemption for the forgiven. A Church that distinguishes between the Holy Spirit and the Church may in faith, obedience, and hope place all trust not in itself but in the Holy Spirit. Thus the Church which proudly identifies itself with the free Spirit of God, with all its presumed strength is really weak, and with all its pretended freedom is really unfree. The Church, however, that humbly differentiates itself from the free Spirit of God is one which, with all undeniable weakness, is really strong, and with all apparent lack of freedom is really free.

Thus we believe *in* the Holy Spirit (*credo in Spiritum Sanctum*). In contrast to that, we believe *the* one, holy, Catholic and apostolic Church (*credo unam, sanctam, catholicam et apostolicam Ecclesiam*). We do not believe *in* the Church; we never really believe in ourselves. We, the Church, believe in the Holy Spirit, just as we believe in one God. With this belief in the Holy Spirit, the one, holy, Catholic and apostolic Church is best provided for. It is the free Holy Spirit that in freedom also liberates the Church to freedom: "Where the Lord's Spirit is, there is freedom" (2 Cor. 3:17).

God's Spirit Works Where and When He Wishes

1) *The free divine Spirit precedes the Church:* The Holy Spirit is not an accident added to the Church as if the Church could also be a Church without the Holy Spirit, although perhaps only in an

incomplete and lifeless manner. If, in Scripture, the Church is called a spiritual building, the temple of the Holy Spirit, that does not mean that the Church is a form, shape, or frame which must be imbued with the Spirit to have life. The Church, therefore, is by no means something that a few efficient and clever ecclesiastical organizers, administrators, and managers could arrange and form so that the Holy Spirit *then* would find, as it were, a place to land, or work, or rest.

Rather, it is the Spirit of God who in freedom *creates* the Church, creates it from among those who believe: "It is only by the Holy Spirit that anyone can say, Jesus is the Lord" (1 Cor. 12:3). By the working of the Spirit, the Church is created and is renewed every day: *emitte spiritum tuum—et creabuntur!* There is no Christian existence that is not *created* as such, and does not have to be re-created continuously; but none comes into being without the working of the Spirit. There is no Church that is not *created* as such, and does not have to be re-created continuously; but none comes into being without the working of the Spirit. To be sure, there is no Church without the free assembling and the decision of the faithful. But the faithful who assemble for the Church do not call themselves together. Indeed, they do not even call themselves to belief. God himself calls them through Christ's word in the Holy Spirit to belief, and so to the Church as the community of believers. God, in the Holy Spirit, does that in complete freedom. The beginning remains with him, as do the continuation and the end. Everything remains with him who, in the freedom of his power and strength, is the sovereign Lord of the Church.

2) *The free Spirit is at work wherever he wishes:* The Holy Spirit cannot be restricted in his activity by the Church. The Spirit works not only through high ecclesiastical positions, but wherever he wishes: among the whole people of God. He works not only in the "Holy City," but wherever he wills: in every church of the one Church. He works not only in the Catholic

Church, but wherever he chooses: throughout Christendom. And, finally, he works not only in Christendom, but again, wherever he elects: in the whole world.

The Holy Spirit penetrates *every* wall, every church wall as well. It is true that the Holy Spirit dwells in the Church, his temple. Here he reveals himself particularly, inasmuch as in the Church the word of God is preached and his sacraments are administered. But the Spirit of God, although he has his domicile in the Church, is not domesticated in the Church. He is and remains the free Spirit of the free Lord, not only of Rome, not only of ecclesiastical offices, not only of Christendom, but of the whole world.

Here some questions arise. Would not we Christians be somewhat more discreet, candid, and friendly in our opinions and actions when confronted with non-Christian world religions if we were thoroughly convinced that the Holy Spirit as revealed in the Church is the Spirit of the Lord of the whole world, who can work wherever he chooses? Would not we Catholics be somewhat more discreet, candid, and friendly in our judgment and behavior toward other Christian churches if we were totally convinced that the Holy Spirit in whom we of the Catholic Church place, or should place, all our hope, is also the hope and strength of all Christendom, as he wills to be in freedom? And would not we who hold office be rather more modest, candid, and humble in our judgment and behavior toward other Christians if we were absolutely convinced that the Holy Spirit, although certainly promised to those who hold ecclesiastical office, is not reserved to them only, but is the Spirit of God who has been given to all believing and loving hearts, and who is able and willing to work freely in all hearts and minds? The free Spirit works wherever he wishes.

3) *The free Spirit works whenever he wishes:* Certainly the free Spirit of God is not a spirit of despotism, of pseudo-freedom, but of true freedom. He is not a spirit of chaos, but of order, not of controversy, but of peace: not only in the world but also in the Church.

The Corinthians who neglected the order of the Church, under the excuse of their spiritual gifts, had to be told by no less a person than Paul that "God is the author of peace, not of disorder" (1 Cor. 14: 33). Therefore, despotism, disorder, and chaos in the Church cannot appeal to the Holy Spirit for approval.

And yet that does not imply that the Spirit blows when he *must*. One should rather understand: when he *wishes*. No Church regulation, in theory or in practice, for example, forces him to act or not to act. God is absolutely free; he is free even regarding his own freedom. He is so overwhelmingly free that he need not ever fear a commitment. Indeed, he does commit himself: to word and sacrament. But in so committing himself, he does not confirm his being committed and unfree, but he confirms his overwhelming, boundless freedom.

God's Spirit is subject to no other authority than the authority of his own freedom. He is under no other law than the law of his own grace, under no other power than the power of his own faithfulness. Therefore God's Spirit certainly cannot be subject to any authority of the Church, the law of the Church, the power of the Church. God's Spirit is not ruled by Church authority, Church law, Church power. As sovereign, he himself governs and rules Church authority, Church law, and Church power. Therefore, whoever in the Church should think of usurping the Spirit by means of any authority, law, or power must necessarily fail. The Church cannot take hold of the Spirit, cannot "own" him, dispose of him, curtail, guide, nor master him.

The Church cannot do any of this, either through its word or through its sacrament. Further, God binds himself in the Spirit to word and sacrament of the Church. But that does not happen by reason of any Church authority, but by reason of God's freedom; not by reason of any Church law, but by reason of God's free grace; not by reason of any Church power, but by reason of his faithfulness. This means that if he binds himself to word and sacrament of the Church, it is not an obligation for him, but for us. We do not

challenge him, but he challenges us. He demands our unconditional *faith*. Neither the word nor the sacrament work automatically; if they find no faith they cannot function. Those who assume
they can forcibly summon the Holy Spirit with word or sacrament,
but also with authority and law, power and order, lack that very
faith which the Spirit demands of them: that faith, namely, which
does not depend upon their authority and law or that of the
Church, their power and order or that of the Church, but upon God's free grace and faithfulness. Therefore it holds true for the
Church as well that the Spirit blows not when he must, but when
he wills.

Here also a few questions arise. Would not we Catholics, in our
dogma of the sacraments, present our *opus operatum* theory in a
more discriminating and exact manner if we would always start
from the idea that the *opus operatum* cannot force the Holy Spirit
but must submit to him in faith? Would we not proceed with all
our canons and regulations—for instance, concerning sacramental
law—much more cautiously if we would always realize that, so long
as they are meaningful and expedient, these rules can be
understood as a concrete realization of God's demands on us?
(They should not, however, be understood as demands of the
Church on the Holy Spirit, as if he were allowed to act only here
and only thus.) Would we not be more cautious in our judgment,
for instance, of the word and the sacraments of the other Christian
churches—say, concerning the validity or invalidity of their matri-
mony, or their eucharist—if here also we would proceed from the
freedom of the Holy Spirit who blows where and when he wishes,
from the freedom of the Spirit that in many a case makes impossible the certainty of any negative judgment?

The Church must not order and regiment the Spirit. It may pray
and ask: *veni!* To be sure, the Spirit lives in the structure of the
Church; to be sure, he stays with it. But he lives and stays there not
because he must, but out of his faithfulness, because he wills

it. "The God who called you is true to his promise; he will not fail you" (1 Thess. 5:24).

Should we, who are the Church, ever be able to forget that we, although forgiven, are sinners, therefore at variance with God's Spirit, that we are "grieving" him and can lose him? Shall we forget that even our faith, although giving us certainty, is constantly being challenged and threatened, and that all we can do is hold on to the faithfulness and grace of God? Can we forget that it is, therefore, by no means a matter of course that the Spirit stays with us, the Church? Is there anything else for us but to cry out incessantly and penitently not only *veni, Sancte Spiritus,* but also *mane, Sancte Spiritus:* stay with us in your faithfulness, despite our unfaithfulness! The Church has not lost the free Spirit of God even though its members continually fail. That indwelling is not a matter of course, but the miracle of God's faithfulness, a faithfulness which must not be taken for granted, but which must be constantly believed in and prayed for.

4) *The free Spirit is the Spirit of Jesus Christ:* Spirit of freedom, Spirit of grace, Spirit of faithfulness—what do these terms really mean? Where have God's freedom, grace, and faithfulness become manifest? Where but in the word of Revelation, in the *logos,* in Jesus Christ? The Spirit of freedom, grace, and faithfulness is therefore nothing else but the Spirit of Jesus Christ. Thus Holy Scripture, particularly Paul, speaks not only of the Spirit of God, but of the Spirit of Christ (Rom. 8:9), the Son (Gal. 4:6), the Lord (2 Cor. 3:18). Thus, the Holy Spirit is the Spirit of *Kyrios,* the exalted Lord. The Holy Spirit is the earthly presence of the exalted Lord. No one else but the Resurrected himself becomes manifest in the Spirit with his power of resurrection. It is the free Spirit of Jesus Christ who brings about the new creation, who is incorporated in the body of Christ, who gives new life and the resurrection of the body. Thus it is all-important that the Spirit that imbues the Church with freedom is no less than the Spirit of Jesus Christ,

the exalted Lord. In him and through him truth comes to light, as St. John's Gospel particularly shows. Here, the Holy Spirit appears as the "Spirit of Truth" (John 14:17; 15:26; 16:13). It is the free Spirit of Jesus Christ who teaches the Church all truth (John 16:13).

Misunderstanding the Spirit

We must seriously consider this statement, that the Spirit teaches the Church all truth. It has been frequently misinterpreted. It has been misapplied by those who thought they could, with reference to the Holy Spirit, indolently let things remain as they were. It has also been misused by those who, on the contrary, thought, with reference to the same Spirit, that they were free to regard and accept any innovation in the Church as a truth of the Spirit. The former as well as the latter interpret this statement incorrectly.

The first group, the indolent *traditionalists*, who with reference to the Spirit, defend everything that has grown in the Church from the past, overlook the passages which *precede* the one that says the Spirit teaches all truth: namely, that the Spirit continously returns to "prove the world wrong about sin, about rightness of heart, and about judging" (John 16:8), that is, to convince the bad, sinful world, inimical to God. The world, yes, but also the Church, which is in this world and which appears only too often as the Church becomes worldly. To the worldly Church, too, the Spirit must continue to reveal its wrong-doing. He must open its eyes about sin, justice, and judgment: about sin, which fundamentally is unbelief in Jesus Christ; about rightness of heart as shown in the justice of Jesus Christ's conquest of the God-hating world; about judgment that, by the death and resurrection of Christ, has been already passed on the God-hating world. Herein, the Spirit shows his freedom.

The Church—and it is we who make up the Church—has every reason to continue to examine its efforts to adhere to its belief in

Jesus Christ, to live according to his justice, and to rely upon the judgment he has already passed. Again and again, the Church has every reason for penance, for contemplation, for conversion, for reform, and for renewal. The history of the Church is, unhappily, not a continual ascent, a continual improvement. The idea of eternal progress, even when applied to the Church, is an idea of the Enlightenment, not an idea of Christian revelation.

The Church which believes in the free Spirit of Christ, who teaches again and again all truth, knows that the Spirit confronts it again and again with its own sin, with the justice of Christ, and with judgment. It knows that the Spirit in this very manner summons it to renewed faith in Christ, to greater faithfulness to the Gospel, to a more serious life according to his message. In this sense, the Church, under the Spirit, must never permit things to remain merely as they were, but again and again must renew all things in this Spirit who renews the face of the earth and of the Church as well, who is the Spirit of whom it is said: "Behold, I make all things new" (Apoc. 21:5).

The word of the Spirit, however, who teaches the Church all truth is misunderstood not only by all those who believe that, with reference to this Spirit, they can permit things to remain as they were, but also by those others who, with reference to the same Spirit, believe that they can accept any innovation in the Church as the truth of the Spirit. These superficial *modernists* are overlooking the passages *following* that sentence about the Spirit who will teach all truth: that the Spirit "will not utter a message of his own; he will utter the message that has been given to him; and he will make plain to you what is to come. And he will bring honor to me, because it is from me that he will derive what he makes plain to you. I say that he will derive from me what he makes plain to you, because all that belongs to the Father belongs to me" (John 16:13–15).

Therefore, the free Spirit of God does not give the Church any *new* revelations, *new* doctrines, *new* promises, complementing or surpassing what Christ has said. It is not said of the Spirit that he will teach *new* truths, but *all* truth. This really is the basic conviction of the evangelist. The word of Jesus is the absolutely decisive word on life and death: "Nobody has ever spoken as this man speaks," the ministers apologize to the chief priests for not having arrested Jesus (John 7:46). The one who speaks here is not one of the prophets of the Old Testament whose words *at times* are inspired by the Spirit, but one who *continuously* speaks and acts out of union with God. No prophet has absolute importance; prophets appear in succession, one after the other. But Jesus is not succeeded by a new revealer: he has given the revelation of God to the world once and for all.

This revelation is certainly inexhaustible. But the new knowledge that is presented to the Church by the Spirit is not supplementary to and does not surpass what Christ has revealed. It is only a reminder of Jesus' words: the Spirit will "recall to your minds" what Jesus has said (John 14:26); "he will not utter a message of his own," but only say "the message that has been given to him" (John 16:13); he "will bear witness" concerning Jesus (John 15:26). The Spirit, therefore, will not teach *anything new,* but everything that Jesus taught and did will be presented *in a new light* and so become clear only in its proper context. In this sense the Holy Spirit reveals freedom.

The Spirit Draws Attention to the Gospel

The recollection of the Gospel of Jesus Christ on the part of the Church: that is an unmistakable sign that the Church is on the right track today, that it is guided by the Spirit of Christ! The Church does not unrepentantly allow things to remain as they were; it reforms and renews its life, its structure, and its doctrine. Yet at the same time, it does not simply yield to new ideas, but it *turns back to its origin.*

The Spirit who draws attention to all truth bestows the freedom needed for this renewal:

The reform of the *Mass* has nothing to do with any fashionable innovations; the object is to bring to light again the original, frequently hidden and forgotten, meaning of the last supper of our Lord in today's eucharist.

The introduction of the *vernacular* into the liturgy is not intended as any external adaptation to prevailing taste, but the announcement and hearing of the glad tidings in the language of the people, understandable to educated and uneducated alike, as it used to be in the early Church.

The re-examination of the *methods of the ministerial office* is not a question of betraying long approved customs in favor of untested methods, but of the service to the people and communities as demanded repeatedly in the Gospel, a service meeting the requirements of the new, changed times.

All endeavors of today's *theological science* are not concerned with the discovery of new, self-made human wisdom, but with energetic re-orientation to the word of God as it is recorded in Holy Scripture.

All endeavors toward an *ecumenical understanding* among separate Christians and Churches are not a consequence of superficial modern indifferentism, but a new realization of the old hope: "That all may be one."

And this is exactly what the present Pope showed the Church and the world so dramatically when he made his pilgrimage to Palestine: the Church must return to the place whence it started. Back to its source! Back to Jesus! Back to the Gospel! Thus a new reality is growing in the Church again: the *Spirit* teaches *all* truth to the Church! It is not a new truth. It is the *old* truth. But it is the *old* truth *newly conceived*. It is the truth of Jesus Christ in the *Spirit!*

Our task today is not easy, the hazard is great. It demands

not less dedication, but more dedication; not less responsibility, but more responsibility. But we have no reason to be faint-hearted, we have no reason to be afraid. We have rather every reason for joyful gratitude that it has been granted to us, of all people, to live in such a time, a time when Church and Christendom apparently have awakened to new life, to new freedom. Is it necessary to say that the new freedom has been the concern not only of the Council, of bishops, theologians, and priests? The *whole* Church wants to be taught the *whole* truth by the Spirit. *Everyone* belongs to the whole Church. Everyone is called upon in today's hour of decision for the Church, called upon to understand, to participate, to go forth bold and patient at once: in word, in deed, in prayer! God's free Spirit is the Spirit of Christ. He presents us who are the Church with the freedom to which Christ has liberated us. "Stand fast, and do not let yourselves be caught again in the yoke of slavery" (Gal. 5:1).

GRACE AND FREEDOM

PIET FRANSEN, S.J.

Since the day St. Paul wrote to his beloved Galatians: "You see, then, brethren, that we are sons of the free woman, not of the slave; such is the freedom Christ has won for us. Stand fast, and do not let yourselves be caught again in the yoke of slavery" (Gal. 4:31; 5:1), Christians have known that God's grace has bestowed on them a new and true freedom.

Through the course of history, however, this joyful message of freedom has either turned into a very abstract and speculative problem, or worse, has become a motive for scandal to our faithful church people. As a matter of fact, this message of St. Paul was not always understood in the Church. One discovers in a commentary on the New Testament that the mistakenly pious medieval copyists hesitated sometimes to transcribe what they read on their own parchments, and that they prudently tried to correct some of the Apostle's more daring sentences. In the meantime either the too speculative bias of the theologian or the exaggerated religious sensitivity of the simple church people undoubtedly obscured the issues St. Paul was fighting for.

It is a tragic dilemma of our Western world that since Pelagius and the controversies about grace in the fourth century up to our recent debates with modern humanism, over the dividing polemics with the Reformation, with Baianism and Jansenism, that the mere reference to the concept of grace has easily evoked in one's mind a kind of menace, or at least a hindrance to our human freedom, and therefore an implicit denial of our human dignity as persons. At the same time, in our parishes, in our schools and colleges, in our religious houses, in our pulpits and in our churches, and most importantly among many officials of the Roman Catholic Church the very word "freedom" became taboo, a dangerous idea, a way of life thoroughly alien to a true son of the Church.

Consequently we shall divide our paper into two parts. In the first section we shall examine the biblical and dogmatic question of the new freedom in Christ which is given to us by grace. In the second we shall have to consider the very practical question of whether true Catholicism has to fall back on the legalism of the latter Judaism or is to make us free, solely because we were indeed freed by grace as children of God.

I. Our Freedom as Children of God

Whenever one opens a manual on the theology of grace at the chapter which since Augustine bears the title *De gratia et libero arbitro—On Grace and Free Will*—one might wonder why from the first, and almost without further question, both realities—that is, grace and freedom—are thought of as opposed to each other. Of course, we do not wish to pretend that no problem whatever arises. But is it not to be deplored that this famous question about our freedom in grace (one might be tempted to say notwithstanding grace) is the only problem that seems worthy of consideration?

St. Augustine, the Church Fathers, and the great scholastic theologians of the Middle Ages were thoroughly aware that there was a double problem. They even had at their disposal a separate terminology for each: the *Libertas Christiana*, the freedom of the Christian, as the primacy of grace; and the *liberum arbitrium*, the more limited question of our human free will inside the divine moment of grace. If the second question is inevitable—at least the history of Western theology tells us so—the first is without foundation. We think that the problem concerning the relations between grace and nature cannot be solved properly if the answer is not based on the biblical doctrine of the new freedom which Christ bestowed on us with His grace. Unhappily this chapter has mysteriously disappeared from our theological manuals, from our catechisms and sermons, and even more completely from our books on spiritual life and religious perfection.

The psychological reason for this, I think, is, before anything else, anxiety and fear. Fear never produces a climate favoring balanced and comprehensive thought, least of all in theology, because then absolute values and truths are at stake. This makes us the more anxious still. Fear now blocks the harmonious processes of thought, especially in matters of faith and religion.

There are historical reasons for this anxiety. The French philosophers of the eighteenth century defended a new notion of human freedom which exploded into the French Revolution and resulted in our modern democracy. Although the discovery of the basic rights of every person in human society doubtless contained many aspects with which we nowadays fully and unreservedly agree, in those days, unhappily, the general trend of the new movement of ideas which changed the face of the Western world was antireligious, or at least was decidedly antichristian and opposed to the Church; that is, it was anticlerical. The Church itself was partly responsible for this, for it was too slow in realizing the impact and the truth of this emancipation. The Church was too involved with the established powers of the *ancien régime* to understand readily the call of God speaking in human history. It took some time before the Church realized that this human and democratic form of freedom had some connection, dogmatic as well as historical, with the freedom revealed to us in Christ. Three centuries before, the Reformation had defended another view on human freedom which was not so much inspired by the new philosophy and humanism as founded upon the teaching of the Gospel. The bitterness of the opposition to clerical authority, and most of all the cruel religious wars and persecutions all over Europe, made it impossible for many Catholics to recognize from the first the real biblical truth and to separate this truth from an aggressive radicalism against authority in the Church, a separation which a Catholic could never accept.

It is the fate of our human existence that human thought seems almost unable to master all the various and nuanced aspects of a rich truth especially in a climate of controversy. Probably in our age we needed to face the horrors of totalitarianism to rediscover the true message of the Bible! In our anxiety over the real or the imaginary dangers of freedom we Catholics consented to locking ourselves inside a religious ghetto. There the discipline necessary to a besieged community led us unconsciously toward a conception of Church life which scarcely differed from the legalism which St. Paul was fighting against in his Epistles and which was clearly condemned by Christ Himself.

St. John tells us of a discussion with the Jews about freedom: "And now Jesus said to those among the Jews who believed in him: If you continue faithful to my word you are my disciples in earnest, so you will come to know the truth and the truth will set you free. They answered him: We are of Abraham's breed, nobody ever enslaved us yet; what dost thou mean by saying, You shall become free? And Jesus answered them, Believe me when I tell you this; everyone who acts sinfully is the slave of sin, and the slave cannot make his home in the house forever. To make his home in the house forever, is for the Son. Why then, if it is the Son who makes you free men, you will have freedom in earnest" (John 8:31-36).

We find here a doctrine of freedom, one very similar to that of St. Paul. Freedom never consists in the pure capacity of indulging in whatever fancy crosses one's mind, limited only by the fancies of others. This false conception of freedom was defended during the nineteenth century; it still has its extreme partisans among a few existentialists and anarchists today. Real freedom, however, is the spontaneous creativity of a human person to realize his own truth. The "authenticity" of our lives to which nowadays people are so fond of referring does not result from any unbounded solipsism, but from a sincere and creative fidelity to a man's own truth. Authenticity is the luminous transparency in a given existence of what one really is before God, freely accepted and freely expressed in one's life. In other words, it is the full acceptance of the situation in which we are set by God, an acceptance which by no means remains passive, but which is creative and unique in its genuineness.

In this light every sin is a freely accepted destruction or, at least, a wounding of our own freedom. Sin is the freely intended suicide of freedom. Sin is therefore undoubtedly an enslavement, because, since it is a distortion of the real situation in which we all stand together before God, it freely surrenders the best of ourselves, our own truth, to alien and lower powers which tend to destroy it. Freedom is therefore truthfulness, faithfulness, and, because of these, authenticity. Only with these does freedom grow freely into ever deeper freedom. Sin is deceit and sham liberty.

Here we discover another characteristic of human freedom, itself the fundamental quality of human existence as such. Freedom never comes to us as full-grown, adult creativeness but is given to us as a risk-fraught and daring adventure, as a splendid human task in fulfilling which we must freely grow toward an ever deeper, fuller, and more ample freedom, an ever more transparent authenticity. We are called to freedom rather than being empowered with freedom or set up in a completely free human situation. This growth toward an ever more mature and adult freedom through a deeper integration of our personal commitment is, of course, a personal calling to the corporate venture of a whole community in this world and in human history as well. The deepest reason for this concept of freedom is that our human existence is an existence in time, and therefore in history, an existence in evolution, in growth, one in which personal involvement remains inseparable from corporate development into the full maturity of the community of men.

If this degree of development holds true for every existence as such, it does so all the more for existence in grace. The reality of grace has been revealed to us both as a corporate existence of the People of God in Christ through the moving and inspiring power of His Spirit, and as institutional growth into the fullness of love. And love, being the very soul of freedom, is at the same time the final and decisive word for grace. There is no richer summary of the doctrine of grace than the formula used by St. Augustine: *"Quia amasti me, fecisti me amabilem*—Because Thou lovest me, O God, Thou hast made me lovable and capable of love." These words have no other meaning than this: Because Thou lovest me, O God, Thou hast set me free!

Actually St. John reveals to us a much deeper mystery. Our freedom, the freedom of which we now speak, never becomes ours, never comes into our own private possession as mere individual enrichment. Grace, too, never becomes our private possession; it is a real life of love ever flowing out of the divine depths and bringing us back to God. It is a living participation in the ebb and flow of the Trinitarian life. Our freedom never becomes ours alone, as grace never does. Our freedom, therefore, says St. John, is the freedom of the Son, the Son of God, because by grace we partake in the obedience and love of the Son for His Father through the inspiring action of the Holy Spirit. Therefore it is the Son "who sets us free" according to His own truth.

Now truth, that is, *aletheia*, has in John's writing a well-defined meaning. John never thinks of the Greek notion, which is rather intellectual: the conforming of one's mind to reality. He uses in the Semitic sense the word *emet*, which signifies a sound and solid foundation, faithfulness, and, finally, a concrete rule of life. Christ is our Truth, because His own earthly life is indeed the glorification of His Father, which means the visible manifestation of the majesty of God, of His *chavod*, His "glory." But at the same time this visible life of Christ shows us the real pattern, the living rule and meaning of life in Christ. This is the Truth which shines in His earthly life, the concrete rule of *our* life, the form of our new freedom.

But this Truth which is Christ is brought to life and to perfection by His own Spirit: ". . . the truth-giving Spirit, when he comes, to guide you into all truth. He will not utter a message of his own; he will utter the message that has been given to him; and he will make plain to you what is still to come. And he will bring honour to me [which means again that He will manifest and reveal and make visible in human history the fullness of God's majesty and holiness, His *chavod*] because it is from me that he will derive what he makes plain to you. I say that he will derive from me what he makes plain to you, because all that belongs to the Father belongs to me" (John 16:13–15).

Recapitulating John's profound theology, we may say: the Father reveals His holiness in His Son, His Logos, the visibility of the invisible Father. Christ therefore becomes our own Truth. But it is the Spirit of the Son and Father who leads us to the full realization of this Truth, the Spirit "who makes known to us" what the Father has revealed in His Son. In doing this the Spirit glorifies the Son, bringing into life and light the sonlike and godlike Truth of the Son, and we in turn glorify the Spirit and the Son, manifesting in our lives what the Father has worked in His Son through His Spirit. But all this is nothing else than our life in grace, our life in the "obedience of faith" and the fullness of love.

Therefore John tells us: in doing this "the Son sets us free." Our freedom is the very freedom of the children of God. Speaking of faith, John reminds us of another of Christ's statements: "Nobody can come to me without being attracted towards me by the Father who sent me, so that I can raise him up at the last day. It is written in the book of the prophets, And they shall all have the Lord for their teacher; everyone who listens to the Father and learns, comes to me" (John 6:44–45). We are indeed directly and inwardly

taught by the Father; this is precisely the divine witness in our
hearts of God's indwelling, reaching into the very depths of our
personal existence; it is what grace truly means.

In his first Epistle, St. John writes: "We are ready to trust
human authority; is not divine authority higher still? And we have
that higher authority for this; God has borne witness to his own
Son. The man who believes in the Son of God has this divine
attestation in his heart; the man who does not believe in the Son
treats God as a liar; although God himself has borne witness to his
Son, he has refused to believe in it. And what is the truth so
attested? That God has given us eternal life, and that this life is to
be found in his Son. To keep hold of the Son is to have life; he is
lifeless, who has no hold of the Son of God" (1 John 5:9–12).

Here indeed we have arrived at the very heart of our freedom in
Christ, a doctrine which—we must confess it humbly—we have
forgotten, neglected, and what is worse, feared and distrusted.
There is a divine witness of truth in the very depths of our hearts,
of our consciences, from which spontaneously and abundantly, as
from a never-drying well of grace, flows the life of our freedom as
children of God. Surely that is our Christian faith. It is the Son
who sets us free, and this new freedom of ours, this freedom of
grace, has no other inspiration, no other strength, and no other
source than the witness, the strength, and the life of the Son
revealing Himself through the power of the Spirit.

St. Paul never proposed any different doctrine on grace and
freedom. In the eighth chapter of his Epistle to the Romans, the
fundamental chapter of the Pauline doctrine on grace, Paul works
out the same theological view. "Those who follow the leading of
God's Spirit are all God's sons; the spirit you have received is not, as
of old, a spirit of slavery, to govern you by fear; it is the spirit of
adoption, which makes us cry out, Abba, Father. The Spirit himself thus assures our spirit that we are children of God" (Rom.
8:14–16).

We notice first of all that Paul clearly condemned this "spirit of fear and anxiety" to which I referred earlier, and which might so easily lead us into a new legalism. St. John was fighting the same enemy when he stated: "God is love; he who dwells in love dwells in God, and God in him." From this statement he immediately concludes: "Love has no room for fear; and indeed, love drives out fear. . . . The man who is still afraid has not yet reached the full measure of love. Yes, we must love God; he gave us his love first" (1 John 4:16–19).

In this passage of the Epistle to the Romans which he repeats in the Epistle to the Galatians (Gal. 4:6–7), St. Paul affirms, as did St. John, that our freedom partakes of the freedom of the Son before the Father, that the Spirit is moving and urging us inwardly toward an ever fuller freedom, and finally, that the source of this sonlike freedom rises from our "heart," the Semitic word for what we would now call the very center of our personal existence and responsibility, soul and body, mind and will, the totality of ourselves confronted with the totality of the reality which rests in God.

This is the common doctrine of the New Testament, one which we have distrusted because we let the spirit of fear, which is indeed the spirit of slavery, creep into our hearts. This anxiety, which we find among bishops, priests, and laymen of our Church, reveals a dangerous suspicion underlying fear, of freedom and personal initiative and creativeness. We distrust, in fact, the very work of the Holy Spirit, and prefer the seemingly surer, safer, and more comfortable solidity of a law which tells us clearly and without "charismatic nonsense" what we have to do and to omit, even what we have to think and to say. If we think about it in full sincerity, this is a tragic form of clerical Pelagianism.

The doctrine of freedom proposed by St. Paul has, as we have seen, the same dogmatic foundation as that of St. John. Paul, however, drew from his profound inner conviction conclusions which are not to be found in John's writings, but which undoubtedly agree with the general attitude of Our Lord as depicted in the synoptic Gospels.

We all know that Our Lord condemned the Pharisees almost exclusively. He showed Himself rather mild and astonishingly forbearing toward the kind of sinners against whom we are now thundering from our pulpits, especially offenders in sexual matters. Did not Christ pronounce these puzzling words: "Believe me, the publicans and the harlots are further on the road to God's kingdom than you" (Matt. 21:31)? We know how He treated the woman detected in adultery and accused by the doctors of the Law (John 7:53–8:11). Luke preserved for us as a treasure the most moving story of an anonymous woman, living an immoral life, who came to anoint Our Lord's feet in the house of Simon the Pharisee (Luke 7:36–47).

It would be naïve indeed to imagine the Jews in Jesus' day as leading an almost angelic life. Especially in the north, in the towns and villages of Galilee, the moral, or rather the immoral, influence of the neighboring Hellenistic towns is not to be underrated. And still, although Our Lord unhesitatingly proclaimed a standard so high for any Christian marriage that even the Apostles were discouraged and objected: "If the case stands so between man and wife, it is better not to marry at all" (Matt. 19:10), His real fight was against the Pharisees. "You hypocrites, it was a true prophecy Isaias made of you, when he said, This people does me honour with its lips, but its heart is far from me. Their worship of me is vain, for the doctrines they teach are the commandments of men" (Matt. 15:7–9; Is. 29:13).

From the biblical stories which we heard as children in catechism class we came to imagine the Pharisees as a very unpleasant, even wicked caste. The paintings we have seen by Christian artists of the Middle Ages and later confirm this childish image, quite untrue to history. The Pharisees were pious people, a kind of religious élite in Israel who dissociated themselves from other Jews

who had accepted a compromise between Judaism and
Hellenism—hence the origin of their name, which means "the
separated ones"—and who strove for radical purity and orthodoxy
in the religion of their fathers. The Gospel tells us, in fact, about
some Pharisees who were pious and sincerely dedicated to their
Jewish faith.

In the course of history, however, Judaism turned into a quite
different religion from the faith of the Hebrews. Certain very
dangerous trends existed within this religion, trends we can recognize in any other religion as the menace to any form of religious
attitude. Back in Palestine, after many decades of exile in alien
countries, the Jews tried to restore their religion on the foundation
of the Law, the Torah, and this Torah became the religious symbol
of their faith. In itself this might not necessarily have endangered
their religion had not the Torah at the same time been turned into
a national and almost racial symbol of election. This was a dangerous shift toward a merely nationalistic and, therefore, purely man-
centered conception of the meaning of religious faith.

This happens, as we said before, in every religion. It is, as history
shows us, the fundamental danger for every faith. Religion means
the full human expression, in social symbols, rites, and attitudes, of
our fundamental relation to God in faith and love. God's majesty
and exacting holiness are intensely uncomfortable and unpredictable. Man, on the contrary, wants safety, comfort, and order. God
asks for our hearts, for total devotion, for a personal commitment
in faith and love unlimited, undivided, and unrestricted. Therefore
man looks for a compromise between his God and his own ease.

There is no better compromise than the safety of the Law. The
Law with its clear-cut regulations gives us the sense of order, of
discipline, of safety and comfort we require. We know exactly what
we have and shall have to do, and thus do not need to think about
it any more. We discern the bad people from the good, the right
answers from the false, the meritorious actions from the sinful.
Living according to the written Law, we know exactly where we

stand—that is, on the good side, and this is indeed a comforting feeling.

But at this very moment a more dangerous and pernicious feeling creeps into our hearts. The only source of sin is pride and selfishness. A hidden pride attaches itself to the correct observance of the Law; we are not only safe, but proud. We can feel we are indeed considerably better than others, and we now begin to despise them. Finally, we turn against God Himself and consider Him as being indebted to us. We imagine ourselves as being in possession of determined rights and claims on God because we have correctly observed His Law.

This attitude is the death of every religion, because in assuming the attitude of self-righteous claimant we set ourselves against God's majesty, indeed place ourselves almost on the same level with Him. A very odd phenomenon, and one which may easily be observed in our own Church, is that wherever legalism prevails one also perceives a tangible increase in juridism, in unbending moral harshness and stubborn religious fanaticism, thoroughly alien to the spirit of Christ, although the people affected by these qualities are convinced of being the most faithful members of the Church, the truest servants of the Lord. Such intellectual and moral fanaticism breeds a paranoiac disregard for the concrete human situation and creates an abstract and cunningly arranged world of principles and values unrelated to reality. Finally, this attitude, called "an unhistorical orthodoxy" by Michael Novak in his book *The Open Church*, generates a dangerous lack of sincerity in which the world of things we ought to do takes the place of the world of things which really happen. Non-human because fundamentally irreligious, legalism under whatever form it happens to force itself upon any society of men is finally the death of the real freedom which God has given us with His grace.

We have constantly referred to an "attitude," because it is precisely this way of thinking which determines the evil nature of legalism. There is, of course, no doubt that God's Law does oblige in conscience. St. John wrote without hesitation: "Loving God means keeping his commandments" (I John 5:3), and St. Paul, who fought so fiercely to retain freedom in the Church, affirms solemnly: "The law, to be sure, is something holy; the ban is holy, and right, and good. . . . The law, as we know is spiritual"; that is, given by the Spirit of God. He continues, however: "I am a thing of flesh and blood, sold into the slavery of sin" (Rom. 7:12–14). It is not the Law which is evil, nor the observance which is sin, but the way we use it, the attitude which governs and determines our obedience.

St. Paul was probably more aware of this critical and decisive difference than the other Apostles because he himself, as he wrote to the Galatians, once fully complied with this conception of Jewish piety (Gal. 1:12–14). Luke, in the Acts of the Apostles, reproduced the speech St. Paul gave to the Jews when he was accused in Jerusalem: "Brethren and fathers, listen to the defense I am putting before you. . . . I am a Jew, born at Tarsus in Cilicia and brought up in this city; I was trained, under Gamaliel, in exact knowledge of our ancestral law, as jealous for the honour of the law as you are, all of you, today. I persecuted this way to the death, putting men and women in chains and handing them over to the prisons" (Acts 22:1–5). And the following day he told them very clearly: "Brethren, I am a Pharisee, and my fathers were Pharisees before me" (Acts 23:6).

When he stood up so decidedly for the cause of Christian freedom, he did so because in meeting the risen Lord on his way to Damascus he had discovered a freedom he never before suspected. But most of all, in the course of his life as a Christian he had found out why Christ Himself condemned almost to the exclusion of condemning others that attitude of legalism in which St. Paul had been born and trained.

In the Epistles to the Romans and the Galatians, St. Paul expressed his new insight into the doctrine of Christ in Old Testament terms adapted to the understanding of his readers. Summing up the central idea of his Epistle to the Romans, he wrote: "But, in these days, God's way of justification has at last been brought to light; one which was attested by the law and the prophets, but stands apart from the law; God's way of justification through faith in Jesus Christ, meant for everybody and sent down upon everybody without distinction, if he has faith. All alike have sinned, all alike are unworthy of God's praise. And justification comes to us as a free gift from his grace, through our redemption in Jesus Christ. God has offered him to us as a means of reconciliation, in virtue of faith, ransoming us with his blood" (Rom. 3:21-15). Linking it up with what he had just written, St. Paul reveals the deeper religious motivation for his conviction: "What has become, then, of thy pride? No room has been left for it. On what principle? The principle which depends on observances? No, the principle which depends on faith; our contention is, that a man is justified by faith apart from the observances of the law" (Rom. 3:27-28). And in a moving final chapter on the purpose of God in history he repeats, in speaking of God's election, that the Jews were selected by the grace of God. "And if it is due to grace, then it is not due to observance of the law; if it were, grace would be no grace at all" (Rom. 11:6). Therefore we are saved only by faith. In a previous chapter St. Paul has told us the reason: "The heart has only to believe, if we are to be justified; the lips have only to make confession, if we are to be saved" (Rom. 10:10).

In stressing the central importance of faith, St. Paul was not thinking so much of the faith of which we write in our manuals of theology, where faith is given a more restricted and technical meaning, but of the decisive commitment to Christ of our whole person, in obedience and love. This faith has been given to us by grace, and it flows from the very depths of our "hearts," the Semitic term for the central core of our person in which true freedom originates.

St. Paul, however, had no illusions about our callousness in distorting the right doctrine of the Gospel. He knew that his doctrine of Christian freedom might be misinterpreted as an invita-

tion to license—this has happened several times in the history of
the Church whenever the Spirit and His gifts were taken as an
excuse for personal selfishness. He concludes his teachings to the
Galatians with this very practical and extremely useful advice:
"Yes, brethren, freedom claimed you when you were called. Only,
do not let this freedom give a foothold to corrupt nature; you must
be servants still, serving one another in a spirit of charity. After all,
the whole of law is summed up in one phrase, Thou shalt love thy
neighbour as thyself; if you are always backbiting and worrying
each other, it is to be feared you will wear each other out. Let me
say this; learn to live and move in the spirit; then there is no danger
of your giving way to the impulses of corrupt nature. . . . Since we
live by the spirit, let the spirit be our rule of life" (Gal. 5:13–16,
25).

Trying to solve a special moral problem for his Corinthians, he
proposes to them the same principle to enlighten their spiritual
discernment: "I am free to do what I will [note that Paul never
denies the central truth of his message—we are free indeed]; yes,
but not everything can be done without harm. I am free to do what
I will, but some things disedify. Each of you ought to study the
well-being of others, not his own. When things are sold in the open
market, then you may eat them, without making any enquiries to
satisfy your consciences; this world, as we know, and all that is in it
belongs to the Lord." Then he writes this marvelous conclusion:
"In eating, in drinking, in all that you do, do everything as for
God's glory. Give no offense to Jew, or to Greek, or to God's
church. That is my own rule, to satisfy all alike, studying the
general welfare rather than my own, so as to win their salvation" (1
Cor. 10:22–26, 31–33).

We may now conclude the first part of our argument. In the
New Testament, grace means before everything else God's saving
love and mercy for every man, which were revealed in Christ and
realized by His divine Spirit—the "grace" we usually have in mind
when we use this word has only a secondary and derivative meaning. The New Testament grace is that new faith and love which

spring from the very depths of our personal existence as the fruit
and the result of the living Presence of the Holy Trinity in our
hearts.

But love is the soul of freedom, and a new love is the soul of a
new freedom. For love is creative, spontaneous, genuine, and personal. This freedom is an ever-new gift of the Holy Spirit. It never
freezes or coagulates into our personal possession, because it is a
life, and not a thing, not a neutral power or an indifferent dynamic
capacity, but life "in Christ, with Christ, and through Christ" by
virtue of His Spirit.

Through the power of the Spirit indwelling in us we partake in
the freedom of the Son, who being fully divine is at the same time
and because of His divinity so intensely human and free. Our
freedom is intensely human, too, because it is born and sustained
by the living presence within us of the divine Persons. Our Christian calling is a calling to freedom, because our Christian law is
nothing else than the Law of Love.

At the end of our argument we must repeat what St. Paul wrote
at the beginning of his letter to the Galatians as he prepared to
propound his doctrine of freedom: "I am astounded that you
should have been so quick to desert one who called you to the grace
of Christ, and go over to another gospel; this can only mean, that
certain people are causing disquiet among you, in their eagerness to
pervert the gospel of Christ. Friends, though it were we ourselves,
though it were an angel from heaven that should preach to you a
gospel other than the gospel we preached to you, a curse upon him!
I repeat now the warning we gave you before it happened, if anyone
preaches to you what is contrary to the tradition you received, a
curse upon him!" (Gal. 1:6–9.)

II.   A Few Practical Questions

This gospel of Christ, so outspokenly proclaimed by the great
Apostle of the Gentiles, is clear enough. But there is no doubt that

we, and many Christians before us, have experienced innumerable difficulties in connecting and integrating this doctrine with the Church's doctrine concerning authority.

We can only intimate here the doctrine of the nature, the source, and the varied forms of authority in the Church. In this matter the fundamental doctrine of Our Lord is equally clear and stands unchallenged. We find its shortest and most pregnant expression at the end of St. John's Gospel: "Once more Jesus said to them, Peace be upon you. I came upon an errand from my Father, and now I am sending you out in my turn. With that, he breathed on them, and said to them, Receive the Holy Spirit . . ." (John 20:21–22).

For the benefit of the Christian converts from Hellenism, Luke and Matthew translated the current Semitic formula "Whoever will receive you, will receive me," an expression we meet in the three Synoptics in describing the mission of the Apostles as: "He who listens to you, listens to me; he who despises you, despises me; and he who despises me, despises him that sent me" (Luke 10:16).

Finally Christ Himself confessed unhesitatingly: "Do not think that I have come to set aside the law and the prophets; I have not come to set them aside, but to bring them to perfection. . . . Whoever, then, sets aside one of these commandments, though it were the least, and teaches men to do the like, will be of least account in the kingdom of heaven; but the man who keeps them and teaches others to keep them will be accounted in the kingdom of heaven as the greatest." But Matthew immediately adds a specific correction to show where the difference lies: "And I tell you, that if your justice does not give fuller measure than the justice of the scribes and Pharisees, you shall not enter into the kingdom of heaven" (Matt. 5:17–20).

The position of Christ, if we see it against the historical background in which He lived and spoke, is clear. There is no other way of salvation than obedience to the will of God, which might eventually find its valid expression in the observance of the written

Law; but this obedience ought to be fully different in quality and nature from the form of obedience of most of the Pharisees. It ought to be the obedience of free men whom Christ has set free, not the obedience of slaves.

How is the Christian paradox possible? How can we live according to a rule which seems contradictory in its wording—that is, where liberty is taken away as soon as it is bestowed? To understand this we first have to restore a richer and fuller conception of the Church, a conception unhappily more or less distorted during the last centuries when we were living and thinking in our Catholic ghetto.

The Church has a double structure: a hierarchic and a charismatic, or prophetic, structure, that is a vertical structure of authority descending from the Father through the Son and His Spirit, and so further through His ordained ministry; and a horizonal structure of spiritual charisms according to which the moving inspiration of the Holy Spirit is given to all members of the Church, without exception. The terms "vertical" and "horizontal," although currently in wide use, are not entirely felicitous. We prefer the biblical distinction between the inward witness of the Trinity in our hearts and the outward witness of authority in the Church, both equally inspired and supported by the same Spirit.

This would appear to be a new paradox, one more baffling if possible than the former. The only way to solve this apparent contradiction, or at least this tension between one's conscience and ecclesiastical authority, is resolutely to think of the authority of the Church in the way Christ saw it and founded it; that is, as a *diakonia*, a ministry, which means a service of authority. The ordained ministers of our Church are the servants of the community in so far as they are indeed sent by Christ to help its members and to guide them in finding God, in meeting Him in their concrete life with the full dedication of their hearts. But they are even more the servants of Christ and of His Spirit in so far as their authority never becomes their own private possession but must be kept as purely as possible open and receptive to the guidance of the Holy Spirit.

On the practical level we are now considering, this means that the exercise of ecclesiastical authority is necessarily linked with the obligation of maintaining a sincere and open dialogue with all the members of the People of God. As long as we retain the essential difference between the office and duty of real and binding authority on one side, and the obligation to discern the voice of the Spirit through an open dialogue on the other side, there is indeed no danger of distorting the doctrine of Christ. If it is true that during the last centuries we have stressed the role of authority to the neglect of the role of the dialogue, there could now be a serious danger that we might emphasize the importance of the dialogue and endanger the holiness of sacred authority in the Church. *But a danger never destroys a truth.* The fact that a real danger exists ought only to warn us that we might misunderstand, in theory as in practice, the real doctrine of the Church. A warning points out the necessity for prudence, but by no means changes a truth into a lie.

No member of the Church could think himself exempted or excused from listening to the voice of the Spirit wherever He might be heard in the Church. No member of the Church, bishop, priest, layman, can boast that he possesses the monopoly of this spiritual guidance. Therefore, for the communion in life and thought of the whole body in a brotherly dialogue it is important to let the voice of the Spirit be fully heard in the Church. But wherever there is a need for an act of authority, *this* ministry is given only to those members of the Church ordained for this service and *diakonia*. It is true, of course, that the grace of the Spirit was also promised to the ordained ministry, but there is no text in the Gospel nor in the true tradition of the Church which tells us that *only* the ordained minister is guided by the Spirit.

Even in extraordinary cases, where the Church speaks infallibly, the final decision of the supreme *magisterium* of the Church never comes about independently from the universal witness of the whole Church. The First Vatican Council condemned only the typical Gallican or conciliar theory, according to which decisions of the Pope had to be approved by the juridical act of a council. This is, of course, a heretical view, because it makes the papal primacy void and false. But the juridical approbation of the decrees of the Pope by an ecumenical council, which the Gallicans were thinking of, is something quite different from the real communion in faith and charity which supports the Pope in his final authoritative decision. This conclusion is, of course, unintelligible to people who represent the Church as a society exclusively based on juridical relations between those in authority and those who are simply its members. Only when we see the Church primarily as a living community, bound together by the mystical motion of the Holy Spirit, are we indeed able to see how a decision of a pope or a council grows into maturity through the various prophetic channels of the Holy Spirit which finally result in an act of authority. This final act may, of course, also be considered as a juridical act of authority, for it lays down a pontifical or a conciliar decree. But before and behind this final act of jurisdiction there is the full reality of the communion of the faith.

But let us consider this organic and complex reality from the point of view of any member of the Church who has to live according to the freedom of the children of God, and who refuses to repudiate his fundamental attitude of obedience toward the holy will of God, as expressed by ecclesiastical authority. This is indeed an eminently practical question. We must first remember the two fundamental truths which are actually two aspects of the same existential reality. The will of God we are thinking of in this connection is first of all not an abstract nor a general rule of law, but one that is intensely concrete and real. It is uniquely *that* which God wants *me* to do in *my* concrete situation. Consequently our conscience, listening to the Word of God, is always concerned with a concrete and practical form of obedience. The

other aspect of the same reality is that God is not so much interested in one's external obedience and one's conformism as in the
absolute sincerity of one's own heart. The will of God determines
an eminent I-Thou relation, as it is called in modern philosophy,
a relation between two persons, between the holiness of God and
one's own personal love of Him.

Therefore the sanctuary in which this obedience originates is
one's own conscience. Nothing is so sacred and final as the human
conscience. There are, of course, many means to find out what God
wants one to do, but if one's obedience ought to be his own, ought
to be free, ought to be Christian, ought to be the obedience of a
child of God, one has no other final instance than the court of his
conscience. This view is basically founded on God's eminent respect for our freedom. No authority, not even the authority of the
Church, can take from me this burden, this duty before God, can
excuse me from this final, personal, and free decision of my own
conscience.

In certain cases, to be sure, one might not see or understand why
God asks one something quite definite through the Church, but
even this so-called "blind obedience" results from the profound
conviction of one's faith and one's conscience as well that in such
matters, otherwise rather limited and well determined, God speaks
to one through His Church. "Blind obedience," therefore, in the
sense of a total or partial repudiation of one's own responsibility for
God, in the sense of mechanical or military obedience, is not
Christian. But "blind obedience" in the sense of a living faith in
the guidance of God through His Church is indeed truly Christian
and free. In that case one's conscience is illuminated and guided by
faith and by love of the Church, the Bride of Christ.

There is another truth which helps us to understand the complex
duties of our own personal conscience. No one doubts one's fundamental incapacity in the course of one's personal life. This is not
only a question of sin, but a question of human nature. In the
words of John Donne, "No man is an island, entire in itself; every

man is a piece of the continent, a part of the main." Actually, to discover the truth about everything, even to live according to our human nature, we all are dependent on one another. Our human existence is indeed a corporate existence which has grown into maturity throughout the course of history. We are dependent not only on our contemporaries, but on our fathers and grandfathers, and we are now preparing the moral and religious future of our children. Therefore the responsibility of our conscience is indeed a sacred charge which we have received in common, a common heritage we carry on together, even when it remains our most private—or, better, our most personal and truly inalienable—duty and calling. It is the same with our freedom. We are free *together*, because we are free as persons, and from our personal freedom grows our corporate freedom expressed in the living community of men. Whenever we stay alone, wherever we separate ourselves from our brethren, we allow our freedom to be mutilated, our conscience to be obscured. Again, the basic reason for this is that God guides us as a person and as a community as well. *We never stand alone before God.*

This human togetherness is before everything else founded in the unifying act of God's creation, in His unifying Presence through grace and providence in our common history, in the unifying guidance of the Holy Spirit, partly expressed in and through the unity in faith and morals in the Church. Once again we meet the dialectical relation, eventually the dialectical tension between person and community. God, who had made us different persons in the unity of the human family, who has by His grace and redemption restored this unity of the elected People of God on earth, does respect the work of His hands, does love the redeeming and saving work of His Son. Nobody in this world has such a delicate respect for and such an enduring patience with the nature of our life and freedom as God Himself, who created and saved us, and who forever remains true and faithful to His word and deeds. God does

not destroy humanity by grace. He makes humanity thereby all the
more human.

Therefore we must listen to the witness of the Spirit, the everlast-
ing source of our freedom in Christ before the intimate court of our
conscience (this the theologians commonly call the internal witness of the Spirit) and to the same witness as proclaimed with
authority in His Church (and this we call the external witness of
the Spirit). Both forms of spiritual witness, of course, have at the
same time an internal and external aspect, but those terms are
chosen to express the dialectical exchange between the inner personal responsibility and the public authority in the Church of
God.

Both "spiritual" realities and their mutual interdependence, it
should be noted, have as their result the freedom of the children of
God, not as a separate entity or characteristic, but as a qualification
of any member within the People of God on earth. The source of
our freedom, as we have insisted, is the internal testimony of the
Holy Spirit, which is actually one of the many aspects of the
richness we discover in the life of grace. When we think about this
fact there is indeed urgent need for a thoroughly new re-reduction
of our Church people, priests and laymen alike. We have to be
taught and trained again in the delicate art of what the medieval
writers called the "discretion of spirits." We have to learn again
how to discern from the many complex, unequal-in-value, and
often obscure movements of the mind and the mood, the authentic
motion of the Spirit in the "heart." This inward motion of the
Spirit toward God gives us peace, confidence, joy, patience, quiet-
ness, and generosity. These are the signs called by St. Paul the
"fruits of the Spirit" by which this motion may be recognized in
the normal development of one's inner spiritual life.

The external testimony of the same Spirit in the Church has a
specific part to play in shaping and ordering the concrete forms of
our free acceptance of the will of God and the inner guidance of

the Spirit. As we have said before, the Church's task is indeed a real
ministry of the Spirit. She has to guide us toward God, not toward
herself. She is not God, but His humble servant, and therefore the
servant of men. She is not the final goal of our life, but the ordinary
and common and most normal way to Christ in this world. The
Church, therefore, was given to man to purify, to keep under
control, and to enrich the limitations of one's conscience, continuously endangered by sin and the consequences of sin.

We have now described the nature of our freedom, the spiritual
forces which support it, and the various misconceptions which
might pervert the authenticity of our free Christian commitment.
We have further reminded ourselves of the existence of a sacred
authority in the Church founded by Christ Himself, and of the
dialectical structure of this ministry which is implied by His divine
institution as being both a competent authority and a service, a
service of the people and, even more, of Christ. We have begun to
analyze the nature of the will of God as concrete and real and as
addressed to every person in particular according to his own situation. Finally we have stressed the crucial importance for valid
moral life in the Church of our personal responsibility before God.
A Christian is a man who follows his conscience, illuminated both
by the teachings of the Church and by the inner light of the faith,
both of these sustained, guided, and confirmed by the divine
illumination of the Spirit.

Our last question is: how can we be both obedient and free,
how can we be both the servants of the Lord and the children of
the Father? This is indeed our problem, and a very practical one at
that. We shall start our answer with a primary question about the
nature and meaning of the will of God as the object of our free
obedience, then conclude with the question of obedience to the
Church. The important point in answering this question is to
maintain a truly religious and not a legalistic approach; that is, to
see the will of God in His own perspective, not in ours. We are
accustomed, I am afraid, to look at the will of God in a rather

external and negative way. When we consider God's will, we see nothing else than the many things which are forbidden and the many things which are imposed on us. This is not in accord with the way God speaks in the Bible, in our hearts, or in the true doctrine of the Church.

It is true, of course, that the Old Testament tradition of the Decalogue might seem to confirm us in this view. But already the Hebrews were being guided by God toward a more religious conception of obedience to Him under the influence of the reform of the seventh century before Christ expressed in the "Law of Sanctity" (Lev. 19–16). In this Law there is a decisive and meaningful command: "You must be men set apart, as I am set apart, I, the Lord your God" (Lev. 19:2). The prophets, who came after, stressed this Word of the Lord emphasizing more than older writings of the Bible had done the personal responsibility of every member of the People of God.

This deep religious motive for all moral life was assumed by Christ, and at the same time fundamentally renewed inasmuch as He presented Himself as the living image and example of the holiness of the Father. The real meaning of the Sermon on the Mount (Matt. 5:7) finds its true explanation in the words of Christ: "But you are to be perfect, as your heavenly Father is perfect" (Matt. 5:48). This is indeed the key to those chapters about which so much has been written. Our forgiveness is inspired by the Mercy of our Father (Matt. 6:12, 14–15; 7:1–2). Especially our love, so strong that we love our enemies, has no other motive than this: "That so you may be true sons of your Father in heaven, who makes his sun shine on the evil and equally on the good, and his rain fall on the just and equally on the unjust" (Matt. 5:45).

Further, according to Christ and His apostles, there is for a disciple of His no other law than the Love of God and of neighbor: "On these two commandments all the law and the prophets [the Hebrew way of naming the Bible] depend" (Matt. 22:40; Mark 12:31; Luke 10:25–26; Gal. 5:22; 6:2). Some moralists, I know, find this too vague for a solid and sound scientific system of moral theology. Their stand is unfortunate, because herein lies the solution for most of their problems. Why is a Christian honest, why does he not kill his enemy, nor leave his wife and children? Because evil things happen to be forbidden? No, but because he has learned to respect the people his Father in heaven has chosen as His children. But even when this view might seem somewhat too abstract, too impractical, the New Testament tells us more, especially in St. John: *Christ is our Truth*. What does this mean? According to the language John was using, "truth" here means a solid foundation and rule for our moral life. In other words: Christ Himself is the visible manifestation of the holiness of the Father whom we are invited to follow and to imitate. This is "the sound foundation" of our Christian morals.

Unhappily in the course of the last centuries a distinction was introduced which deprived this Gospel doctrine of its full meaning and impact. This distinction was used especially in connection with the Sermon on the Mount and similar teachings of Christ. For whenever one reads these pages of the Gospel with a legalistic bias in mind, one is left at a loss. One's common sense suspects that it is not always possible nor advisable "to turn the other cheek," "to pray in the secret of the inner room"—why, then, have churches as we do?—nor "to sell everything and follow Christ." At the same time one perceives that Christ was talking quite seriously. Thus theologians and spiritual writers have introduced the convenient distinction between the Law of the Decalogue, meant for the people living in the world, and the so-called "evangelical counsels" taken from the Gospel, meant for the life of perfection within a religious order. We do not deny that religious life is indeed inspired by the Gospel, but as a principle of interpretation of the Gospel this distinction is useless.

The "Law of Holiness" was promulgated for *all* followers of Christ, without any exception at all. But it is not a law as human laws are: abstract, inflexible, and compulsory in their full meaning after proper promulgation. Yet it would not be adequate to hold that Christ was talking in terms of flowery language, as Orientals did and still do, for the meaning of the images and the parables is clear enough. They doubtless suggest a radicalism, tempered by Christ's divine mercy.

If we would know how God's will addresses us, we have only to look at Jesus, the image and the Word of the Father among us. His demands for moral perfection and holiness are limitless, absolute, and utterly radical; they frightened even His apostles (Matt. 19:10). Nevertheless we do not recognize in His attitude either the paranoiac rigidity of a fanatic or the juridical abstractness of a judge, nor, finally, the petty stubbornness of an ignoramus.

One of the most revealing stories of the Gospel is the parable of the lost son (Luke 15:11–36). But Christ did not restrict Himself to telling charming stories; He enacted them as well. Consider the occasion when He met the young man who was very rich (Luke 18:18–24; Matt. 19:18–30), according to Mark's account: "Then Jesus fastened his eyes on him, and conceived a love for him. In one thing, he said, thou art still wanting. Go home and sell all that belongs to thee . . . then come back and follow me. At this his face fell, and he went away sorrowing, for he had great possessions" (Mark 10:21–22). One notes a similarity of context with the woman taken in adultery (John 8:3–11), with the sinful woman who anointed his feet in the house of Simon, the Pharisee (Luke 7:36–50), or with Zacchaeus, the chief publican in Jericho (Luke 19:1–10). "That is what the Son of Man has come for, to search out and to save what was lost" (*ibid.*:10). Their sins receive no approbation nor excuse, but the sinners find mercy and forgiveness.

Never do we meet in Him that kind of sentimental chiaroscuro in moral matters which nowadays we consider the ultimate form of tolerant humanism. Christ was utterly, shockingly intolerant, but at the same time so humiliatingly understanding and patient that He leaves our fashionable tolerance far behind. To say that sin is not sin and good is not good, that both are fairly similar when one takes the trouble to look at the complex subconscious motives of our actions, is neither tolerance nor understanding. That is not to deny that we do suffer from deeply placed psychological tensions. But if we are to be taken seriously, not as playgrounds for conflicting complexes but as responsible persons truly emerging from the purely mechanical or instinctive urges of their psyches, then there comes a point in our lives when we must call a sin crudely a sin and good forthrightly good. It was because Christ took us seriously that there was such understanding and mercy in His divine radicalism.

In endeavoring to understand humanity the first thing one has to accept is that man never received freedom, full grown and mature, as a Pallas Athene, springing full armed from the head of Zeus. We are called to freedom, and we freely grow into freer freedom. As we have seen, this is true for the individual and also for any community of men. Therefore the first quality of our understanding and tolerance is patience. When we know what it is to be human, we will wait for time, and still more time, to let things ripen and mature. Everything in man is subject to the law of growth, not least his moral sense and morality, and much more, his insight into Christian perfection.

God knows the work of His hands. He can wait. Christ, the Word of the Father, could wait, too. He waited until after His death to send His Spirit. He is still waiting, because we in the Church are still far from the divine perfection of the Gospel: "But you are to be perfect, as your heavenly Father is perfect" (Matt. 5:48).

Dogmatic theology and the history of salvation reveal to us the same wonderful mystery of God's absolute call to holiness and His merciful patience and fidelity. Theology tells us that man was called to grace from the very beginning of his existence on earth, and that God never withdraws this initial invitation to grace and love. But what does any life of grace really mean? It means that the Holy Trinity is dwelling in us, inwardly inviting and attracting us toward a Godlike life of love, partaking in the radical and absolute obedience and love of the Son for the Father through the virtue of the Spirit. This radical requirement of divine perfection is so inherent in grace that without it no grace is left.

This grace was offered to the first men, to the Hebrews, to the Jews, to the peoples all over the earth, to the Christians in the Church. That is the history of our salvation, and this history has already covered some twenty thousand, if not a million, years. And God has waited lovingly, forever faithful to His first love. The absolute radicalism of the inner call to grace has never abated, as God continues patiently to move and steer peoples and individuals, saints and sinners, toward the full divine perfection which was revealed in Christ.

That is how God's will addresses itself to man!

If this be true, and our faith tells us that it is, then we see how fully free we can be in our utmost obedience. Our obedience first proceeds from grace, that is, from genuine love, inspired by the motion of the Holy Spirit: ". . . the love of God has been poured out in our hearts by the Holy Spirit, whom we have received" (Rom. 5:5). Second, God's call reaches us, as we have already seen, in the concrete situation in which we actually exist. God is drawing us from where we stand, albeit in a state of sin, ever nearer to Him. He takes into account our weaknesses, our anxieties, our timidities, our selfishness; He does not let us drown in our own miseries, but helps us out of them. Here we think of the moving words of Newman, when, in Sicily, he was himself in a state of physical misery and spiritual despair: "Lead, Kindly Light, amid the encircling gloom, Lead Thou me on!" Third, what God wants is our heart. Nothing else. Therefore He will always call for the creativeness, the genuine initiative of a sincere and authentic commitment. His only Law is: Follow Me! This was repeated again and again by Christ Himself: "Come, and follow Me," from where you stand, just as you are, but follow me sincerely, leaving everything which is not Me behind. The only thing that does not belong to God is what is against Him, what is refusing Him, what is affirming itself as an idol before and against God, that is, our selfishness and human pride.

When we look at the lives of the saints, including the lives of many unknown people who were never canonized by the Church although they led lives of deep and loving perfection, we may see from the very variety and richness of those lives what it means to listen to God's call in the spirit of freedom. We may think of Thomas More, the chancellor of England and friend of many learned contemporaries; of Benedict Joseph Labre, the despised beggar and squalid pilgrim; of the magnificent archbishop and cardinal of Milan, reformer of the Church, Charles Borromeo; of the poor and not-so-learned parish priest, Father Vianney, Curé of Ars; of Elizabeth, duchess of Thuringen, mother of three princes; or of the young peasant girl, Maria Goretti, who died for the sake of purity. Kings and peasants, scholars and soldiers, mothers and nuns, all bore witness to the radicalism of their Lord, and followed Him with the genuine, almost poetical creativity of a great love. Were there ever men and women so free, so independent, and so unique, sometimes so nonconformist as well? And at the same time was not the driving power of their lives precisely their utmost obedience to the inner voice of the Spirit, calling them to follow Christ, and "to be perfect, even as your heavenly Father is perfect"?

That is what Christian perfection means. But how, then, does it happen that a Christian has seemingly to live among so many interdictions and bans? Very often we pity ourselves, thinking with sad resentment of the "freedom" possessed by people who have no faith or conscience to worry them.

To think in this way is to show that we have indeed a wrong conception of Christian morals. Our moral education at home, in our schools and colleges, and, I am afraid, even in our Catholic universities, is frequently inspired by the strongly legalistic approach to moral theology of the last centuries, and has told us only of as many interdictions as there are different kind of sins. But we are guilty, too, because our lack of love of God leads us to look at those commandments from the wrong side. We are like children, crying because our mother takes away from us a bottle containing a bright red liquid, which happens to be poison. We are like the mad, egomaniac drivers who swear at any traffic rules, but forget that every year about 150,000 of their own countrymen in the United States—husbands, wives and children, friends and lovers—are killed on the streets, more than in many battles of human history.

We must never forget that the so-called negative aspect of God's will, the many prohibitions and "Thou shalt not's" of which we complain, do not primarily come from God, but are motivated by our own sinfulness. It is because we, not *God*, can allow hate to overflow our hearts that we are told not to kill. It is because *we*, not God, can misuse that unique institution of love, Christian marriage, on which God has set so fair an image of His own intimacy within the Trinitarian life, that divorce, adultery, and the many distortions of marriage which we have invented are forbidden.

In other words, the interdictions and bans of Christian moral theology are only *secondary* aspects of Christian morality. They are by no means central, and therefore they are incapable of inspiring, in the true sense of the word, true Christian morals. Moral theology has to be built on dogmatic truths taken from the Bible, from the tradition of the Church, from the saints. It is not clever casuistry about the question of how far we can go to avoid either mortal or venial sin. Moral theology belongs to dogmatic theology, is an integral part of it. It follows the same methods. It is not a kind of extension of Canon Law, which uses completely different methods, at least in regard to matters which fall under strictly ecclesiastical jurisdiction.

Thus we come to touch on the laws of the Church, a final question. As we have seen, the Church has received from Christ the sacred authority to lead us in His name. She has therefore the right and the duty to speak in the name of God. How are we to understand the laws of the Church, how are we to accept them, and nevertheless remain free? I have just stressed a crucial point in this matter in saying that moral theology is not to be separated from sound and authentic dogmatic theology. Both have the same object, the saving reality of God, as revealed in Christ. Both use the same sources for their knowledge: Holy Scriptures and the tradition of the Church. Both have the same purpose: to know better the ways to our salvation, and so bring us nearer to it. Both, finally, have the same method, that is, reflection on the substance of God's Word.

But moral theology, like dogmatic theology, is only a part of the living tradition within the Church. The theologians, it is true, have their own task in safeguarding the divine heritage of Christ. But the other members of the Church are not to be left out of this. Just as they have to bear witness to their faith in living communion in the same faith with all other members of the Church, they have undoubtedly to bear witness to the true Christian conception of moral life in the same communion of love and faith with other members of the Church. In dogmatic theology, in the texts of the councils and the popes, "faith and morals" are put and kept together.

"Faith and morals" both come from the same revealed truth, the first pertaining more to our salvation as it comes to us from God, the second more to that same salvation as it has to be actualized in everyday life. I would certainly not think of saying that the first is theoretical and the second practical, for both depend on an eminently practical question: our common salvation in grace. Dogmatic theology which is not at the same time a spiritual theology, inspiring our daily life, remains arid and lifeless speculation. Moral theology which is not founded on the fundamental dogmas of our faith remains arid and lifeless casuistry.

What I have to say in conclusion will remain completely pointless and useless unless our moral theology and at the same time our whole Christian moral education is not fundamentally reformed, rethought, and built anew upon a more solid and more Christian foundation. Nevertheless, in safeguarding the sacred heritage of Christ there is, as we know, within the Church a third mission—we have already referred to the ministry of the theologian and the laity—the ministry of authority, as it was founded by Christ and entrusted primarily to the world episcopate in communion with the Pope of Rome, and in a subsidiary way to the priests ordained as collaborators of the bishops. Theirs is the task of exercising religious authority, and inevitably this authority has great significance when we are considering the morality of our lives.

What is the role of the Church in determining the inspiration and the shape of Christian life? And how can we be fully obedient and at the same time remain truly free as children of God?

The ministry of authority in the Church has a double task or mission. Our bishops have first to safeguard our faith, to defend it. When such necessity arises, they have to determine with authority the true formulation of our faith. With regard to the morality of Christian life, their task is absolutely the same as for the defense of the faith: to *keep safe* the heritage of sanctity entrusted by Christ to the Church. Second, they have to *govern* the People of God in human history as a religious community of men.

The bishops have first to defend the "Law of Sanctity" to which we have referred before, to explain it, to purify the various human interpretations of any misconception or fraud, that is, to *keep safe* the true structure of Christ. In this they are infallible as regards the defense of faith, or within the same limitations as are accepted in theology in connection with dogmatic teachings.

Therefore the case of our obedience and freedom is not intrinsically different from what we said in explaining the true nature of the will of God. The Church has indeed primarily to propose the *positive* will of God: "Be you perfect as your heavenly Father is perfect." For the same reasons, the Church has consequently and secondarily the duty to warn against and eventually to forbid every action which intrinsically could bring about the destruction or

denial of that holiness and which is fundamentally *in opposition
to the love* that God is offering us in grace.

Most people think only of this secondary task when they look at
the Church. As a matter of fact, it could happen that popes and
bishops, since they are human as we are, and therefore influenced
by their time, their education, their immediate entourage and its
mentality, are more preoccupied with bans and excommunications
than with the preaching of Christian perfection. This has happened in history, and it could happen again.

In accordance with this mission, the Church has to interpret the
divine will to the People of God and to apply it to the ever-
changing circumstances of life. When she tells us that something is
a mortal sin, she is saying only that a certain action or omission is
fundamentally *a refusal of the love of God*. For sin is nothing else.
The Church, however, is never able to declare that such and such a
man is living indeed in a state of mortal sin. Our only Judge is God.
The Church's only mission is to enlighten and guide our consciences, to warn us that in a determined case, a certain kind of
action is intrinsically opposed to the will of God. I have earlier
called this the external witness of the Church.

We agree with many other theologians in thinking, moreover,
that the Church is not qualified to make into a mortal sin—that is,
"to forbid under pain of mortal sin"—something which is not so in
the eyes of God. This question was brought up by several bishops at
the third session of the Second Vatican Council. The answer
depends fundamentally on what one accepts as a definition of
mortal sin. Wherever the notion of mortal sin retains the juridical
aspect which was attached to it in the last centuries—namely, is
defined as an action opposed to a kind of divine decree and which
excludes one from heaven—it might be possible to think that the
Church might declare some action to be a mortal sin which is not
so in itself. But to one who holds a more theological and existential
notion of mortal sin—ontological if one dislikes the word
"existential"—this is unthinkable. Actually moralists have been

known to make such declarations—but they are not infallible. I
know a professor of moral theology who, having revised and repub-
lished a manual of moral theology written by his predecessor,
boasted of having done away with about sixty mortal sins! It is clear
that at least one or both were wrong—the man I met or his
predecessor.

The sacred authority of the Church is meant only to safeguard
the truth, that is, the Truth of God. It is this Truth that she has to
defend, to proclaim, to interpret, and, if necessary, to define by a
solemn act of the pontificate or the conciliar *magisterium*.

This is not always so easy as it might seem to one who is unaware
of the riches and the depth of divine Truth and of the complexity
of human life. We are thinking now of the serious reflection and
study which at the moment are going on within the Church
concerning the urgent but difficult problem of birth control. That
our modern Church, confronted with the complexities and the
variety of questions arising from this problem, still refuses to make
a final statement is only a proof of the prudence and wisdom of the
bishops who now govern the Church. They are indeed inquiring
into God's will in this world situation.

In this paper we have criticized a certain predilection for casuistry which can be found in the moral theology of the last centuries. It would be inane to refuse place to any casuistry at all in
these matters. It is clear that the many aspects of human life
demand a nuanced and qualified answer, especially in matters so
important for our daily life as those treated by moral theology.

There is a second ministry of authority in the Church: to govern
the People of God in human history. The Church is not a democracy; that is to say, the source of her authority does not rest in the
consent of the people. Her authority comes from Christ, the King
and Lord of human life on earth. But even if the source of this
form of authority is indeed a mission from Christ, the exercise of
this authority is human. On this level the Church is infallible
only within the limitations which are explained in theology;

namely, the Church is unable to make universal laws which are
directly opposed to "faith and morals." Apart from this restriction,
the value of these laws is strongly dependent on the spiritual
wisdom and prudence of the ecclesiastical legislators. There are
good and less successful ecclesiastical laws. These laws have continuously to be reformed and adapted to new circumstances of life, as
is happening now following the Pope's announcement of the ap-
pointment of a special commission for the reform of Canon Law.

As members of the People of God, "fellow citizens [who] belong
to God's household" (Ephesians 2:19), we revere and love the
superiors Christ has given to His Church, remembering St. Paul's
words to the leaders of the Christian communities, the so-called
presbyteroi: "Keep watch, then, over yourselves, and over God's
Church, in which the Holy Spirit has made you bishops; you are to
be the shepherds of that flock which he won for himself at the price
of his own blood" (Acts 20:28). Holding them in reverence, we
follow their guidance and obey their prescriptions.

But this we have to do in a spirit of freedom and not in a spirit of
anxiety or lip service, as children of God and responsible members
of our community. Therefore we obey, not because of any penalty
attached to disobedience or merely to avoid whatever mortal or
venial sin might be involved, but out of a spirit of faith and love.
For we believe that the Spirit, that same Spirit who illuminates our
consciences, is also guiding them, so that they—or at least the
living community of bishops all over the world in unity with the
Pope—are unable to lead us astray from the true path of "faith and
morals." We love them, moreover, as visible images of Christ, the
Head of the Mystical Body. For the bishop is really the image of
Christ, or, as Oriental Christians say, "the Icon of Christ."

Our freedom further manifests itself in sound Christian maturity. One of the characteristics of this adulthood in faith is that we
are able to distinguish the central truths, the "so-called substance
of our faith," from the secondary truths, the divine will in itself
from the exercise of human ecclesiastical authority in virtue of a

commission given by Christ. We never confuse the Word of God and the word which is spoken in the Name of God. No bishop is an "incarnation" of the Spirit!

If the divine will is eternal, inaccessible, and absolute (in the sense we have seen before), the Church's ordinances as expressed in Canon Law, in the decrees of the popes, and of the Roman congregations, in the ordinances of any bishop in his particular diocese are subject to change and open to reform; since they are inspired by human wisdom and prudence they are only "negatively" (as the theologians say, and within the limits indicated in theology) preserved from error. Therefore it is perfectly permissible for us, as responsible members of our Church, to strive for a reform of certain laws and ordinances that are outdated or insufficiently adapted to concrete circumstances, each of us acting according to his calling, talents, and experience.

Our maturity will also express itself in the way we consider these laws, in the ways we interpret them. Of course the Code of Canon Law comprises laws which are the expression of divine institutions and ordinances, but in this context we are considering only such laws as are strictly ecclesiastical.

The Code of Canon Law and the juridical tradition of the canonists, their jurisprudence, contain the most important principles of interpretation. *And it is neither a sin nor an imperfection to follow those principles approved by the Church herself.* It seems quite useless to make such a statement, but experience shows that even some bishops ignore this.

Every law that is a prohibition of something has to be interpreted strictly according to the meaning of the formulas and words used, *and it is no sin to do so.* Every law conceding a privilege or a favor has to be interpreted in the most benign way possible (*within the wording of the law,* of course), *and it is no imperfection to do so.*

In extraordinary circumstances not foreseen by the law no law obliges in conscience, *and again it is neither a sin nor imperfection to consider oneself excused.* In important things it is only wisdom to consult a prudent man, but not necessarily a priest.

It is clear from what we have said that the methods of interpreting the laws of Canon Law and the methods of finding the will of God in moral theology are intrinsically different. That is the reason moral theology should be completely separated from strictly canonical studies and methods, and integrated, as it was in former times, into dogmatic theology. The methods of the two are fundamentally different, except for those cases where both sciences may happen to overlap. A mature layman should have a fairly well-grounded insight, or at least a practical one, into the fundamental differences between the two. Legalism originates precisely from the confusion between moral theology and Canon Law.

This "sense of distance" regarding specifically ecclesiastical laws should never threaten our "sense of obedience." This happens only within a childish and immature mind. Christians of this kind, and unhappily they are quite numerous, cannot imagine the existence of any real obligation as soon as the penalty of mortal or venial sin is removed. That the will of a superior really binds our consciences, without its disregard necessarily inflicting on us the penalty of sin, is normally unthinkable for men and women, priests, and bishops educated in a strongly legalistic religiosity. When we get to the root of the matter, the image they have of God is—unconsciously, no doubt—the image of a super-policeman, knowing everything, noting down everything, forgetting nothing.

In other words, our attitude of reverence, love, and obedience toward the Church is a moral question; the way we interpret the canonical laws of the Church is a juridical question. This attitude makes it impossible any longer to *overemphasize* the obligation of Canon Law, something which is frequently done because of the unhappy confusion between moral theology and Canon Law. At the same time one will never *underemphasize* the absoluteness, the radicalism, the purity, and the holiness of the divine will, which is a common fact of experience, and for the same reason.

Our freedom as children of God is possible only with a mature and adult insight into our faith, and with a mature and adult insight into the moral and ecclesiastical obligation of our consciences. In this sense we may truly contend that Canon Law also belongs to the economy of grace, because it is fundamentally the manifestation of God's same loving care through the ministry of the Church. But this grace, as all other graces, is not given to atrophy or to suffocate the freedom we received in Christ. In the Christian religion grace is freedom, because both are founded on the truth, the Truth of God. Life in grace, freedom, and Christian obedience are not contrary to one another: all are expressions of the new wisdom.

In the words of the Apostle Paul: "Who else can know a man's thoughts, except the man's own spirit that is within him? So no one else can know God's thoughts, but the Spirit of God. And what we have received is no spirit of worldly wisdom; it is the Spirit that comes from God, to make us understand God's gifts to us; gifts which we make known, not in such words as human wisdom teaches, but in words taught us by the Spirit, matching what is spiritual with what is spiritual. Mere man with his natural gifts cannot take in the thoughts of God's Spirit; they seem mere folly to him, and he cannot grasp them, because they demand a scrutiny which is spiritual. Whereas the man who has spiritual gifts can scrutinize everything, without being subject, himself, to any other man's scrutiny. Who has entered into the mind of the Lord, so as to be able to instruct him? And Christ's mind is ours" (1 Cor. 2:11–16).

THE FREEDOM TO BE HUMAN

WILLIAM F. LYNCH, S.J.

I have found several times—and therefore I will do it again—that if I propose an image or central picture as I begin to write—an image that will save me from abstraction and that will light up a few sentences that would never otherwise have had light, that somehow things go better and not worse. Call it a composition of place, if you will—but there is no reason why a law of good writing should contravene a law of prayer—so I will have at least an initial image—and I will ask the reader to use it and to keep coming back to it.

In this case it is taken from a novel by a German-Jewish-Bohemian writer, Franz Kafka, who was born in 1883 and died in 1924.

The image is the image of a castle and a set of townspeople who live below and around it. The natives have an unbounded will to live in tune with the ruling castle. How shall we please it? What is its will? What is the one thing that is right? When will it be satisfied? There is no direct way of getting in touch with the castle, so that you are largely on your own, to find, in every situation of many possibilities, the one magic way that will dispel the fog and make that castle smile.

God forbid that the people should fall back on their freedom! Remember the problem of the townspeople with regard to the castle: "Whatever one does, it is always wrong."

And there is the eternal hope of K, the leading character, that he will find the one right way in any situation—that is made for him and he for it.

Philosophically we will call the castle the pure object.

And with this image in mind I shall have at my subject.

I

I should like to make this a study in the relations between the freedom and the humanity of man. I think that for modern man there is an equation between these two things, between his freedom and his humanity.

If I set to an immediate explanation of how and why I think that this is so, I will at the same time be giving a focus and an orientation to these pages. For my wish is that they should deal entirely with this equation. At the same time I shall be developing a parallel concept. That will be the relationship between the several forms of what I can call mutuality, on the one hand, and freedom and creativity on the other.

Our equation between freedom and the human does not so much mean that it is human to be free, though there is obviously a good deal of truth, to put it mildly, in such a statement. But, after all, there is a sense in which we can say that it is without substance. I mean that the proposition—thus stated, to be free is to be human—has no body and is without flesh and blood. For such a proposition surely leaves us in a floundering state, wondering what freedom is and wondering how one should go about this business of being free. Whereas the reverse proposition—namely, that where we are human we are free, and to the degree that we are human we are free—will turn out to have flesh and blood if it turns out to be true. For we know less about freedom than we do about the human.

It is indeed right to carry this initial thought one step further and to propose that the center of the modern crisis of freedom for man is his great desire, not that he should be free after the manner of some vacuous ghost, but that he be free to be human. This is his true preoccupation today, and it is what we may call his true theological preoccupation, this right and need to be human. So strongly does he feel about the matter that even if his humanity turns out to possess certain elements of unfreedom, as indeed it does, he will buy it nevertheless, at any price, this fundamental freedom to be human. We very much miscalculate if we decide that his passion is for a ghost or a vacuum, for some metaphysical or absolute freedom. It would be unjust to him to think of him as absorbed in this adolescent dream of always wanting to be free and somewhere else. No matter where or what he would be, he happens to be a man. Others have noted before this that his dreams are adult; he wants something, he wants the human, and he is willing to take a good deal of what goes with it. He is even willing to drink it as a chalice, so long as he may have it and no one will take it away from him.

This is the essential freedom that he wishes; it is his fascination and preoccupation; he thinks of the age he lives in or, at any rate, the age he wishes to live in, as an anthropological age. Compared with this humanity, all other freedoms would be trifles or an idle dream.

Permit me to take the liberty of exploring this equation between the free and the human. By way of doing so I shall ask myself three questions and shall try to propose the beginnings of answers to them.

1. The first question is: What is this thing called the human?

2. My second question is: In what way and sense is the idea of the human a free idea and a creative idea?

3. My third question is: What are some of the major fantasies and nightmares through which this idea must pass before we can pursue it in simplicity, according to the liberty of the children of God?

It is amazing how such simple words as "the human" can frighten many people, including many otherwise sensible theologians. It no longer makes sense to criticize the human, at least as we now think of it. A fact is a fact is a fact, and that is what the human is, a fact. It will do no good to question it, because at the end of all our questioning there it will be. It is our part, our island, of existence.

We are setting out again on a new and yet more daring exploration of this idea of the human. That is one reason why we call this an anthropological age. So our contemporaries will fight two things: a) any dehumanizing process; b) or any theology, or supernaturalizing theory that will question or interfere with the human.

It would be temerarious of me, to put it mildly, if I should try here to give a substantive description of any meaning to the word human in this context. Since Shakespeare himself had only begun to be able to do what I am thinking of, brevity would be in better taste—so that a few guidelines for our context will be mentioned. I mean, for example, and among many things, the freedom of man to develop, in independence and according to his own needs and interests, the great human orders of politics, science, psychology, the arts, and the total life of the imagination. I mean the liberty to hypothesize wider and wider patterns of discovery and to explore them. I mean the freedom of the imagination to imagine new forms, new stories, new interior and exterior worlds of the human. I cannot briefly say all that I mean, but let me say that I do not mean something merely intellectual by the human. Far from it.

We must push the idea of the human as a saving idea into every possible corner. Who is not human? What in us is not human? The schizophrenic has the feeling that he is not human, and many fractions of the human race have this fear. We must, on our part, extend the idea to more people as well as to more ideas.

Once again this does not mean that men will reject anything that interferes with their freedom. It means they will accept nothing and will fight everything that interferes with their freedom to be human. Whether and how much the human is free is another question.

II

Let me mention a number of the central qualities of the human as free and creative.

1. The human is both a definite idea and reality, and an open, to-be-determined idea and reality. What is human is remarkably open to determination, with the sole proviso that whatever comes out of it must be human. The idea and the reality will not be completed until the last man has lived and died, and has had his last thought.

2. In this centrally, this critically important sense the existential proposition is true that the decisions, the history, and the makings of man will determine the idea and reality of man. We will not only explore man, we will create him; although what he makes or what he makes of himself must be human.

3. There are usually multiple choices for man in the real order. It is his choice and his wishing that create the right thing in all such cases. A doctrine of sheer objectivity, a theory that says there is always a right thing to do, always a will of God, always a natural law determinant, closes history and creativity, and would indeed lead to endless scrupulosity and illness.

4. The imagination of the artist produces the new, and is always extending the idea and possibility of the human. He cannot deal with an absolute or an absolute objectivity that would predetermine all and would not leave him his autonomy as an artist, his freedom to imagine the new.

He is professionally afraid of the absolute, but it is we who have made him misunderstand it. He has a picture of the absolute as something that pushes things around from the outside and that predetermines everything and that has already said the last word.

But the most difficult creation of the absolute is the autonomy of man. After all, it is easier to push something from the outside than from the inside. The word human has both the gift and the evil genius for setting up many reverberations. Let me mention a few of them.

For many religious thinkers it means neutrality, noncommitment, the most beautiful and therefore the most dangerous of all the forms of nonreligious life.

For others it means everything that was meant for them by the "humanism" that grew up among us in the twenties and the thirties of this century, a limited humanism that should never be equated with the word human as it is used here.

It is especially necessary to deny that the human, as I use the word and as many today address themselves to the reality, has much in common with this "humanism."

For the gnostic imagination, it means the very devil, it means the work of the devil. For the gnostic, who is the forerunner of the Manichaean, both the created world and the human are a "world of darkness, utterly full of evil . . . full of devouring fire . . . full of falsehood and deceit . . . a world of turbulence without steadfastness . . . a world of death without eternal life."

Nor is it necessary for me to enlarge on the later Manichaean development of these ideas, a century later. Now even more clearly "The human body is of devilish substance and—also of devilish origin and design. . . . This hostility and this asceticism have their general rationale in the gnostic view of things . . . but rarely have they been so thoroughly and so unyieldingly underpinned as in the Manichaean myth." [1]

We shall be soon searching for a principle of freedom that loves the human and that wishes to create the human; but now, for this brief moment, we look at the beginnings and development of a gnostic and Manichaean tradition of freedom that hates the hu-

---

[1] Hans Jonas, *Gnostic Religion*, p. 227.

man and is destructive. And this shall be a good continuing question about the freedom we shall choose from now on in; whether it shall be destructive or creative.

For the long gnostic and Manichaean tradition, the world and the human are objects of hate, contempt, and fear. They must be dealt with by aversion and revolt. Everything about them is an attack on our freedom. It is impossible to be human and to be free, according to this tradition. An American idiom would say that to be free and perfect it is necessary to spit in the eye of the human. When we have done what we wished, when we have torn down and destroyed the human law, then we will be free.

We of our generation, I think, know a good deal more about this counterfeit or simulacrum of freedom than at any previous stage of human history. We recognize the presence in Manichaeism of feelings of entrapment and fear of what we have lately been calling the human condition, and we now know that what looked like freedom was a wild thrashing about in an attempt to escape. And we are inclined to think that what is trying to escape from the human is the omnipotent part of man, or shall we say the child in us that wants to be omnipotent.

In all these formulas of action, therefore, we are more in touch with their inhumanity and their destructiveness, and in them we no longer acknowledge the presence either of freedom or creativity. We may consider this as an accumulation of new religious insights, but, ironically, they were a contribution not of theology but of the new mental sciences.

III

Therefore it seems to me a good assumption or hypothesis to explore, that if we are to find the freedom we are seeking for and if we are to be able to move successfully into the adulthood of an anthropological age, we first establish certain principles of mutuality with the world and with God. Without such a relationship of mutuality we will be neither free nor creative. With it we can and will be both. With it we will have a realistic and nonmysterious foundation for both.

Allow me to develop this hypothesis. And as I proceed I think it will be clear that I will be trying to do two or three central things. I will be trying to suggest a really human and realistic theory both for freedom and creativity. I will be attacking the purely interior and romanticized concept of both. I will be suggesting that, if we would only examine its resources and be a little more confident, we would find that Christianity has incomparable resources for the building of the free and creative city of man.

By mutuality I mean an interacting relationship, or an interacting contribution that occurs between man and the world, or between persons and persons, or between man and God, from which something new and free is born. There are, therefore, two ways in which both the free and the creative involve mutuality.

First, both freedom and creativity involve an interacting contribution. This means that in the making of an object by an artist or in the making of a world by man, there is indeed objectivity but there is no such thing as a pure dominating object or fact to which man and the human would not have given a contribution and some shaping.

Second, where there is an interacting and mutual relation between people such as I have in mind, then those who live within such a relationship and within reality are free with an unconditional freedom to do what they wish, according to the mandate *ama et fac quod vis* (love, and do what you will); and according to the liberty of the children of God.

These are my two planks for the study of the relation of mutuality to freedom and a creative life. Let me elaborate on each of them.

1. Man is increasingly exposed to the many theories of reality as pure object which abound among us. He had been told for centuries that reality was reality, and a fact was a fact was a fact, and a

rose was a rose was a rose, and that it was his business to accept and submit. Obviously there was a good deal to this; especially if one were crossing the street at say Forty-second Street and Broadway where it was obvious that one should by all means avoid all objects that were heavier than oneself. Nevertheless it was also an overfearful and gross exaggeration of many situations in reality, in the life of knowledge, in the life of the arts. In these man has a vital part to play in the construction of reality and the ideas and images of reality. Therefore the older humanism of a generation ago will be too pallid and will not stand the weight of the demands of our generation that man have a greater part in the construction of the real and of facts, that there will be a mutuality between him and the world that will destroy neither the world's objectivity nor his subjectivity.

Certainly this question must be broken down into dozens, perhaps hundreds, of special problems, and all of us will be competent to make judgments in only a few of them.

What shall we say, for example, of the cry of the modern painter that he refuses any more to be bound by appearances but will, instead, make a new reality of his own? This is a special part of the question which refuses to be bound by appearances but requires special knowledge, special judgment. In modern physics there are, I understand, basic questions of this order. Does the presence of the human experimenter obscure or contribute to the situation?

In every ordinary sense impression, a psychologist such as Jean Piaget asks, does man mechanically record appearances with his eyes, or do the eyes help to create the scene? Thus the cry of the painter against appearances becomes a cry of protest against appearances he would have himself created and would like to improve.

These are so many special questions, but there are broader, more effective, and affected human areas where certain aspects of this question emerge with greater simplicity. For example, we know with surety that the balance between the active and the passive is always a delicate and a difficult thing to preserve in the lives of human beings. In our own time, under what pressures we shall see, the balance has by all odds shifted toward the passive and passivity, with all the feelings of helplessness and hopelessness such an imbalance can cause to reverberate in the soul. If this is true, and we think it is, it is the truth of it that explains the great modern counterreactions of search for whatever will make men active, creative, autonomous, and possessed of some sense of human identity, and of their own contributions to reality.

If we should make the simplest possible division of the world into the two things called the *subject* and the *object*, meaning by the one the subject, the full internal reality of the human being and by the other the object, the rest of the universe outside of him, we have the simplest possible picture of the two poles of the conflict modern man conceives of himself as waging. Ideally, of course, there should be no conflict, but in actuality there is. At any rate, there are many forms and areas of life in which it is impossible for human beings to make their contribution to a subject-object relationship. So much shaped by the world, it is impossible for them to shape it in return, to shape it, that is, into their own human forms. They are asked to be passive and to suffer the domination of the object—which is not freedom. They feel that they are driven and not driving.

If men must be creative, as they must, this need of being active shapers of their environment may surely be accepted as one of the most fundamental elements of any understanding of human creativity.

2. We believe, next, that when we talk of that kind of shaping and making and doing that belongs to creativity we are talking of the forming of a *human* world.

The reverse ideas are in the ascendency. When we think of the worlds in which we live or are asked to live, we ordinarily think of worlds with their own laws and their own reality, waiting for us to fit into them and to submit. Obviously, there is a good deal of truth in this image of *the world*. For there *are* thousands of things we can do nothing about and that await our gracious acceptance. But there are thousands of other things that are a parody of this fundamental reality situation. They pretend to stand before us as analogies of God and the unalterable truth and demand our obedience. So far as types of social organization go, this is the very essence of what we call the collective society, whether the types of this society belong to the East or the West. It may also be called the mechanical society or the formal organization.

By mechanical organization we mean a completely preplanned, purely rational, and logical pattern for work or life which is dictated and controlled from the top, which therefore exists with its own life, separately from the lives and needs of its human members; it exists without any shaping or participating decision by its subordinates and uses only some minimal and precise talent of the human beings involved (or caught) in the pattern. It is concerned with its own needs (for example, profit) and not with the needs of men. It is more mechanical than human.

IV

The second form of freedom and the creative that proceeds from our hypothesis of mutuality is thus expressed: *ama et fac quod vis*—over against the gnostic formula: hate and do what you will.

In the gnostic formula there is no relationship, whether of friendship or love, and the free action is founded on spite and the destruction of the first signs of any relation. Actually, it is not free because it is compulsively spiteful.

In the Christian formula: *ama et fac quod vis*, the free man will never violate the relationship of friendship or love, be it with God or man, but it is still more important to realize that such a relationship, correspondingly, will never interfere with freedom. It does not blackmail; it does not establish conditions of love; it does not say that some way is and must be the right way. As long as there is a presence to reality and the relationship, there the freedom among choices is absolute possession without price. Now there is real hope, no matter what happens in the world outside such relationships. For the final object of all our hope is love.

Now, too, we are in a position to "create" our own souls and foster their growth, and to have them created and fostered by another. Real love communicates a self-identity and autonomy that are no longer in basic conflict with real mutuality. It takes two real self-identities to make a relationship, and it takes such a relationship to make two real persons. In mutuality, each of the parties helps the other to become himself. Even if we limit ourselves to that much and no more, it is already clear that such a unity is creative.

Real mutuality communicates freedom. If we remember that mutuality includes a profound wishing together, we may understand how this is so. In real friendship or love, the mutual situation seems to rise in a completely liberating way above the necessity of defining itself by a precise wish that says in effect, cither wish this or there is no friendship or love: Take a trip with me today, or have a drink with me now; do as I wish, there is no bond otherwise. Such either-or situations have two effects: 1) They determine the nature of mutuality, not from within, but from some precise, objective, and limiting fact on the outside. Wishing and wishing together become completely externalized, and what becomes divinized here is not love, but some petty external fact, all-consuming and threatening. 2) This fact, whatever it is, establishes itself as a dominating, tyrannical, demanding condition. It makes mutuality conditional at its heart: if you take this trip with me, I will love you. All mental illness has this deep sense of conditional love.

Not only does this reduce friendship, love, and mutuality to the external and the conditional; very often they become plain, outright blackmail. This kind of relationship, if sufficiently extended, produces some degree of mental illness. It also makes creativity impossible. Creativity, we have noted, may mean many things; but it invariably means, among these many things, that what is brought into the world is completely new, unconditioned, and in contact with the depths of personal thought and feeling and wishing. In all these senses, it is felt to be free.

It should be clear that real mutuality, real love, does what it wishes and allows others to do what they wish. *Ama et fac quod vis.* It seeks a moment that will be internalized, unconditioned, and totally new, therefore creative. Before we reject such a human hope out of hand as absurd, irrational, and dangerous, let us consider this ambition, this reaching for such innocence in wishing with great care.

I propose that (in this critical question of locating the heart of true mutuality) the ideal situation at which Christianity aims is totally removed from the situations that tend, in our day, and in any day, to produce mental illness in a civilization.

In mental illness, the striking, recurrent phenomenon is that of the wish that seems to be wrong, forbidden, judged, condemned. This holds true even for two wishes that form a set of contraries—one of which should certainly turn out to be all right. Mental illness discovers that not only is it forbidden to go for a walk, but so also it is forbidden not to go for a walk. The prohibition and the inhibition have become progressively universal. Most agonizing and most destructive of all, the exterior human figures and situations which originally did the forbidding are now incorporated and literally become psychological parts of the self, so that the self denies, destroys, and inhibits the self. The oppressive system, obviously and essentially noncreative, has been incorporated as an actual, living entity. There is no mutuality between the real self and this incorporated self, and the more the latter prevails, the less freedom there is.

We have seen that in Christianity the terms of human situations are totally different. In terms of illness, everything is forbidden. In terms of Christianity, the only condition is that we observe the limits of good and evil. But this is not a condition as we have used the word condition. Evil is essentially wishing for some form of

nonbeing and the nonhuman; it is best understood as a refusal to
wish the human. Therefore, we can express the freedom of Christianity in another simple form: if the human personality is inserted
into reality, if its choices are reality-choices, then it does not make
any difference what it chooses. It is free, and absolutely free. Let us
be as simple as can be in our examples. It does not matter before
God or man whether we walk or ride, whether we take coffee or tea,
whether we decide to be a doctor, lawyer, priest, butcher, baker, or
candlestick maker, whether, if both are possible, I rest now or work,
whether I continue this sentence or end it here. This is surely a part
of what is meant by the freedom of the children of God, who are no
longer servants or slaves asking the master of the house if this or
that is all right, but are rather children of a Father who communicates family rights and does not question. It is we who raise the
question.

This is the most extraordinary and most fruitful form of mutuality in the world. Granted our presence to reality and to love, God
wishes us to choose, in the knowledge that it is all right to choose
and that choosing and wishing then make the choice the right
thing. This is not subjectivity or solipsism because every choice of
love is related to reality and is the choice of a reality. On the other
hand, neither is it magic—which would be the case if there were
only one choice among thousands which would be the best, and
God help us if we did not find it. The theological supposition that
there is one right way is the ultimate source of all externalism.

This kind of magic has the effect and intention of absolving us
from wishing and thinking, and from all the operations of a truly
interior life. It supposes that there is some one precise, magical
thing or person or event in the world outside us that will happily
come along to do the wishing for us. It allows us to project our
identity, our capacity for thinking and feeling and wishing, outside
ourselves, and so we are left haunted by that sense of a lack of
identity characteristic of all our illnesses.

There are other ghosts to haunt and afflict us. If we insist upon
inserting "morality" into the wrong places, if we insist that there is

one right answer for everything, if we require that the object do all the wishing, without the mutuality of our own wishing, there are ghastly consequences. First of all, the process never works: *it introduces an endless and exhausting search into life.* Pure externalism involves endlessness. Second, no matter what we do within such terms as these, there is a sense of failure and of guilt and of being judged by some anonymous object with which, no matter what we do, we cannot make contact. For this magical object we seek, this one right thing, is really nonexistent; but it exercises a strange and absolute tyranny over everything we do. Because we are not free and because we lack Christian interiority, we are oppressed by an anonymous and ruthless sense of law. The strange myths of the novels of Franz Kafka are full of this sense of constant and anonymous judgment upon ourselves from which we have no recourse, for the guilt cannot be located, and the judge is anonymous, and the judgment without reason. How can such a psychology or theology produce anything but hopelessness?

Clearly there is no mutuality in such situations. The object does all the work. As often as it does, it becomes tyrannous and unfruitful for us. But if we are honest we will recognize in ourselves a secret and powerful wish to conspire with such totally objectified and tyrannous situations, to abandon our own wishing, to give up the burden of our souls. The Grand Inquisitor of Dostoevski was half right. God wishes us to be free, with the freedom of mutuality between subject and object, between ourselves and the world, between ourselves and Him. But half of us rejects this freedom, this mutuality. It is too much trouble.

This is only part of the truth, however. There is also in every man and woman a deep, absorbing desire for identity and for the salvation of which identity is an analogue. This desire is an actual, vital, driving force whose strength we simply cannot calculate. Where it is frustrated it produces the only agony that really matters. If man cannot in this sense create, he feels lost and lost to himself. Rather than being absorbed by biologically dangerous wishes (as we read in the system of Freud) he now refuses to wish or takes the cosmic stance of wishing *against*, because of the failure of his search for mutuality. I agree, therefore, with Dr. Leslie Farber that the probable basis of hysteria is some form of refusal to wish or of wishing *against*. These hysterical roots he summarizes under the name of *willfulness*. We have seen that it is a good word to distinguish the whole world of the willful, the irrational, and the solipsistic from the creative world that I have tried to summarize under the idea of wishing. And we can repeat the words of the angel of God when he said to Daniel: "The Lord hath loved thee because thou art a man of desires."

No two sets of terms can be more unlike than the terms of illness and the terms of Christianity. In saying this, I have no slightest intention of criticizing the sick or of excluding them from Christianity. Indeed, it seems necessary that all of us, in our spiritual history, should pass through this way of law into the life of Christian liberty. But how shall we progress if we do not sense that the terms of the stages differ? To mental illness, all is forbidden and nothing is right. Its final logic is checkmate, the failure of mutuality, and hopelessness. It often involves a struggle to the bitter death between two inner parts of the soul—that which seeks identity, mutuality, freedom, and that which is the very spirit of denial and negation. But to Christianity, once the decision is really made, everything is permitted, anything may be wished, there is no more bowing to every wind from the outside world, there is possession of one's soul, and the possibility of restoring the old idea of the soul as a garden. There are definiteness and rest.

All this is the fruit of mutuality.

We are, then, apparently in the midst of a great anthropological age, wherein man advances toward new heights of creativity, knowledge, mastery, and self-actualization. Perhaps he does not so much fear the power of the atom as he fears his own power for acting and wishing. He does not feel that it is altogether right to wish so much and so greatly. Therefore he stands guilty, not in fact, but in fantasy. He feels that he lives in opposition to the old gods, and does what he does without a sense of mutuality, and with the taste of the forbidden. A superficial theology would be tempted to say that these feelings and fantasies are correct, that man dare not aspire to be God. But why not, why not wish greatly and go forward boldly, if God wills it so? Christianity alone, with this sense of absolute freedom within reality, can take away this anxiety. Within what other terms can man be creative in peace? How can he get through this daring and difficult period successfully without this sense of mutuality? Without this profound assurance that it is all right to grow up and all right to be man? Without the confidence that it is God's will as well as his own?

If man is to be free according to the modes here suggested, he must move through many fantasies, most of them the products of modern history, before he comes to this fact of freedom. The great fantasy or imagined connotation is that he who wishes to become man and to be free is a rebel. This is the major fantasy to be overcome. The major accompanying feeling is that of guilt. These fantasies and feelings, while most sharply expressed since the Renaissance, have a long history. Great literature has expressed them —in the myth of Prometheus, in the theme of *hubris*, in the great stories of Greek tragedy, in the Faust legend. In our own day there is Camus' *The Rebel*. In all of these is one of the strongest strains of Romanticism: that man must come into his own. Behind the search for the human, therefore, there is the burden (but not necessarily the reality!) of hostility, rebellion, guilt.

Let me conclude by recommending the exploration of these two hypotheses:

1. Romanticism set the human project but was not capable of dissolving these burdens.

2. Christianity cannot only acknowledge the human project and the validity, the fundamental innocence of "an anthropological age," but it also has the resources for the dissolving of the heavy burdens of the rebel.

Teilhard de Chardin on Freedom and Risk in Evolution

Christopher F. Mooney, S.J.

The thought of Pierre Teilhard de Chardin is at present open to a number of unfortunate misunderstandings. Not the least of these is the belief that he looked upon the evolutionary process as an inexorable movement of natural forces within which the dignity of the human person and the responsibility of human freedom were somehow minimized or obscured. In point of fact the very opposite is true, and my purpose is to bring some measure of clarity to this particular area of Teilhard's thought. We shall approach our subject on the first two levels only of his evolutionary system, namely the level of his phenomenological analysis and the level of his philosophic option. We shall not attempt to deal with the third level of Teilhard's thought; namely, that of Christian Revelation. This is not because there is nothing to say about freedom on this level, but rather because there is too much to say.

Let us begin, then, with Teilhard's phenomenological analysis of evolution, for this analysis gives us the key to his understanding of the human person. Perhaps what is most striking is that this analysis is his attempt to find on a purely scientific plane a common ground of discussion between "materialists and upholders of a spiritual interpretation, between finalists and determinists." One group insists on talking about objects as though they consisted of only external actions in impermanent relationships; the other group is obstinately determined not to go outside a kind of solitary introspection in which things are looked upon only as being shut in upon themselves in their "immanent" working. Both these groups see only half the problem. "I am convinced that the two points of view require to be brought into union, and that they will soon unite in a kind of phenomenology or generalized physics in which the internal aspect of things as well as the external aspect of the world will be taken into account. Otherwise, so it seems to me, it is impossible to cover the totality of the cosmic phenomenon by one coherent explanation such as science must try to construct." [1]

This plan for an enlarged science faithful to its phenomenal character is at the heart of Teilhard's whole analysis of evolution. In regard to man especially, he never ceased pointing to a modern anomaly in the academic world: both the "materialists" and the "spiritualists" have managed to shut their eyes to the intimate connection between man and the concrete material world, "one group from fear of falling into metaphysics, the other from dread of profaning 'the soul' by treating it as a mere object of physics." The result is that man, "in so far as he has something special to reveal for our experience, that is to say, in those characteristic qualities which we call 'spiritual,' is still excluded from our general constructions of the world. Hence the paradox: a science of the universe without man. We have knowledge of man on the fringe of the universe, but still no science of the universe including man as such. Present-day physics (using the word in the broad Greek sense of 'a systematic comprehension of all nature') as yet makes no place for thought; which means it is still constructed wholly apart from the most remarkable of all phenomena provided by nature for our observation." [2]

Teilhard begins his study of man by insisting upon the interdependence of energy in the world, a fact which up to now science

---

[1] Le Phénomène humain, 1938–1940, Oeuvres de Pierre Teilhard de Chardin, vol. I (Paris, 1955), 49–50. (Eng. trans., The Phenomenon of Man [London and New York, 1959], 53). Hereafter cited as PH.

[2] Le Phénomène humain, 1930, Oeuvres, III (Paris, 1957), 228–229.

has provisionally decided to ignore. He assumes all energy in the world to be physic,[3] although this manifests itself in two different tendencies, which he calls respectively radial and tangential energy. Radial energy tends to draw an element forward into structures of greater complexity; tangential energy, on the contrary, tends to link an element to other elements on the same level of organization. In the early stages of the earth, says Teilhard, it was radial energy which led to the production of larger and more "centered" molecules, until such time as the first "critical point" of evolution was reached and there was the sudden appearance of life.

This presence in nature of critical points finds its most startling application, however, in the case of "hominization," or the instantaneous leap from instinct to thought. Tangential energy had, in the slow course of geological time, continued to cause living cells to reproduce themselves on the same level, but radial energy began immediately to take the form of biological evolution, drawing life forward toward a new critical point. Teilhard insists that the parameter for measuring the relationship between these two energies is the law of complexity consciousness. For him this means that a more developed consciousness will always correspond experimentally to a more complex organic structure of greater internal unity and concentration. The direction of evolution can be judged, therefore, by following "Ariadne's thread," the line of growing complexity, a line which has gradually made its way through mammals and primates up to man. In the primates, Teilhard notes, evolution went straight to work on the brain, neglecting everything else. In their case, consequently, an increase of consciousness is always found to be in direct proportion to the degree of "cerebralization," that is, to the increase in complexity of the nervous system and brain. Through this phenomenon of cerebralization the ascending advance of life was slowly directed toward the critical point *par excellence*, the threshold of reflection.

[3] There is an unfortunate rendering of *psychique* as "physical" in the official English translation of *PH*, page 64 (page 62 in the French).

What Teilhard de Chardin is affirming then, at this early stage of his phenomenological analysis, is that the world is a coherent unity, that a single pattern runs through the whole of the universe, and that this pattern has one orientation and one only toward man. Far from being an exception to biological evolution, man is in reality the key to the entire process. For Teilhard it would be utterly absurd to think of evolution suddenly going off in a direction other than that running from the primates to *homo sapiens*. In this sense evolution is irreversible, although this irreversibility is obviously not absolute, but conditioned on whether or not mankind continues in existence. If it does, then evolution must also continue its single upward movement toward greater consciousness. Consequently to consider man as anything else but the principal aim of cosmic development is unthinkable, not only because he comes at the end of a progressive interiorization of matter moving upward along the axis of complexity, but much more because the phenomenon of reflective consciousness is of its very nature totally unlike any other event in the evolutionary series. Looked at superficially, the "psychical" make-up of various species in the proximity of man seems to reach right up to the borders of intelligence. In reality, however, the crossing of that threshold was a unique event, of an order quite different from that of nonreflective consciousness, "a mutation from zero to everything." [4]

The whole sense of evolution, therefore, must reside in the fact that it is an ascent toward "personality." To use Teilhard's own English expression, we are living in "a personalistic universe." Man alone in the material world can say "I." He alone is a "person," able to communicate with other persons on the level of spirit. Teilhard returns to this point constantly. Consider, for example, the following texts.

The true evolution of the world takes place in the souls of men and in their mutual union. Its inmost agents are not mechanistic but psy-

[4] *PH*, 188 (Eng. trans., 171).

chological and moral. . . . It is not the rigid determinism of matter and of large numbers, but the subtle combinations of spirit, that give the universe its consistency. . . . People usually speak of person as if it represented some quantitative reduction or qualitative diminishment of total reality. Exactly the opposite is the way we shall have to understand person. The 'personal' is the highest state in which we are privileged to grasp the stuff of the universe. . . . The only way to express in a phrase the fact that the world is continually moving forward without loss is to say that the quantity and quality of the personal must constantly go on increasing.[5]

These citations make it clear that for Teilhard the advent of thought represents not merely a turning point for the individual or even for the species, but that it marks a transformation which affects life itself in its organic totality. Properly speaking, from now on the evolutionary process continues its development not so much in the sphere of life, the "biosphere," as in the sphere of mind and spirit, the "noosphere," the "thinking layer," which since its germination at the end of the tertiary period has spread over and above the world of plants and animals. "Even from the most dispassionate point of view possible," says Teilhard, "the phenomenon of man represents nothing less than a general transformation of the earth, through the establishment on its surface of a new envelope, the thinking envelope." Or again: "This sudden deluge of cerebralization, this biological invasion of a new animal type which gradually eliminates or subjects all forms of life that are not human, this irresistible tide of fields and factories, this immense and growing edifice of matter and ideas—all these signs that we look at, day in day out—seems to proclaim that there has been a change on the earth and a change of planetary magnitude. . . . The greatest revelation open to science today is to perceive that everything precious, active, and progressive originally contained in the

[5] Mon univers, 1924, 14; Le Milieu divin, 1927, Oeuvres, IV (Paris, 1957), 173. (Eng. trans., The Divine Milieu [London and New York, 1960], 129); La Crise présente, 1937, published as "Sauvons l'humanité" in Cahiers Pierre Teilhard de Chardin, vol. III (Paris, 1962), 78.

cosmic fragment from which our world emerged, is now concentrated in and crowned by the noosphere." [6]

Up to this point Teilhard's phenomenological analysis has been concerned with the meaning which evolution gives to man. He now turns his attention to the more important question of the meaning which man gives to evolution. For it is of the very essence of Teilhard's thought that the world is still in process of development. There is no reason whatsoever to suppose that the evolutionary forces at work for millions of years should suddenly have ceased to operate once the threshold of reflection had been crossed. The crucial difference, however, is that all subsequent change must henceforth take place on the other side of this threshold, in the noosphere. "How could we imagine a cosmogenesis reaching right up to mind," says Teilhard, "without being thereby confronted with a noogenesis? . . . *The social phenomenon is the culmination and not the attenuation of the biological phenomenon.*" "Noogenesis" will therefore be spiritual and social; that is to say, it will concern itself with the development of individuals as persons and with society on the level of interpersonal relationships. This is "socialization" in Teilhard's sense of the term, a slow process of "collective cerebralization" within which the law of complexity consciousness operates in the same way as it formerly did in the case of individual cerebralization before the coming of thought. "It is therefore a mistake," says Teilhard, "to look for the extension of our being or of the noosphere in the impersonal. . . . In any domain—whether it be the cells of a body, the members of a society, or the elements of a spiritual synthesis—*union differentiates*. In every organized whole the parts perfect themselves and fulfill themselves." [7] The dichotomy between totalization and personalization is the result of confusing individuality with personal-

---

[6] *Le Phénomène humain,* 1930, *Oeuvres,* III, 231; *PH,* 202–203. (Eng. trans., 183.)

[7] *Ibid.,* 244, 247. (Eng. trans., 221, 223.)

ity. "The goal of ourselves, the acme of our originality, is not our individuality but our person: and according to the evolutionary structure of the world, we can only find our person by uniting together.". . ."Totalization and personalization are the two expressions of a single movement." [8]

The primary result of this movement toward what Teilhard calls "socialization" has been that in our own age we have come to constitute an almost solid mass of humanity within which the totality of thinking units is always tending toward greater personal interiorization and greater interpersonal communion. In other words, the law of complexity consciousness continues to be operative; through technology tangential energy produces a more complex exterior organization of humanity, a kind of "megasynthesis," while at the same time radial energy fosters a correlative spiritualization, a further intensification of the psychic temperature of the noosphere. Socialization is thus gradually developing into a "planetization," that is to say, a coiling up of the human species more and more tightly around the surface of the earth.

Here we should note again that we are still, in Teilhard's mind, on the level of phenomena. It is no departure from scientific method to recognize the direction which a trajectory *should* take if it continues to follow a course whose past has already been charted. Teilhard believes he has found a single evolutionary pattern up to the present, and he would seem to be justified in deducing from this the mode of its future development. Evolution has been seen as an ascent toward man and reflective consciousness, and toward nothing else. The formation and deployment of the noosphere continue this ascent. Unless the movement ceases altogether, therefore, it must advance in the direction of a certain harmonized collectivity of consciousness, some ultimate manifestation of radial energy's tendency to bring greater unity from greater complexity. The universe would thus be converging toward some ultimate

[8] *Ibid.*, 289, 291, 292. (Eng. trans., 260, 261, 263.)

point of planetary maturation, still millions of years away, which Teilhard provisionally calls the Omega Point, since it would come at the very end of the whole evolutionary series.

We should also note that up to the present we have been dealing with a hypothesis regarding the *probability* of convergence. The pattern which Teilhard has discovered is, as we have seen, irreversible, but this irreversibility is external and relative. Noogenesis must indeed continue toward some supreme consciousness, but only on condition that it continue at all. And on the level of phenomena we have absolutely no way of knowing whether or not this condition is to be fulfilled. As a phenomenological law, the pattern of complexity consciousness is unable to tell us if the universe is really *destined* in and through man to reach the Omega Point.

This last fact is extremely important, for as we shall see in a moment Teilhard is about to advance from this hypothesis of probability, based on the experimental law of complexity consciousness, to a hypothesis of *actual* convergence, that is to say, to a study of the conditions required in order for mankind to know that here and now it is *actually* converging toward a supreme center. This change of perspective is going to force him to leave the first level of his phenomenological analysis of evolution and move to a second level, that of a philosophic option based on his phenomenological analysis. He himself announces this change of level at the end of the third book of *The Phenomenon of Man*. "Either nature is closed to our demands for futurity, in which case thought, the fruit of millions of years of effort, is stifled, still-born in a self-abortive and absurd universe. Or else an opening exists—that of a super-soul above our souls. . . . On neither side is there any tangible evidence to produce. Only, in support of hope, there are rational invitations to an act of faith." [9] "Faith" in this context has nothing to do with Christian revelation. It is a common Teilhard-

[9] *Ibid.*, 258. (Eng. trans., 232–233.)

ian synonym for "intellectual synthesis" and is explained quite clearly in the following text:

On the strictly psychological plane . . . I mean by "faith" any adherence of our intelligence to a general view of the universe. . . . The essential note of the psychological act of faith is, in my opinion, to see as possible and to accept as more probable a conclusion which, because it envelops so much in space and time, goes far beyond all its analytical premises. *To believe is to achieve an intellectual synthesis.*[10]

Teilhard's act of faith, therefore, is a philosophic option and is, as he himself says, "strictly undemonstrable to science." [11] Its point of departure is the study of two factors, two phenomena, which have profoundly changed the whole character of noogenesis. The first is modern man's sudden awareness of what is taking place in him and by means of him. *The Phenomenon of Man* links the whole psychology of modern disquiet with the confrontation of space-time.

What has made us in four or five generations so different from our forebears (in spite of all that may be said), so ambitious, too, and so worried, is not merely that we have discovered and mastered other forms of nature. In the final analysis it is, if I am not mistaken, that we have become conscious of the movement which is carrying us along, and have thereby realized the formidable problems set us by this reflective exercise of the human effort. . . . What makes and classifies modern man . . . is having become capable of seeing in terms not of space and time alone, but also of duration . . . and above all of having become incapable of seeing anything otherwise—anything—*not even himself* . . . the definitive access of consciousness to a scale of new dimensions.[12]

The result is the "malady of space-time," the feeling of both anxiety and futility, the sense of being crushed by the enormities of the cosmos.

---

[10] *Comment je crois,* 1934, 2.
[11] PH, 316. (Eng. trans., 284.)
[12] *Ibid.,* 238, 243. (Eng. trans., 215, 219.)

Far more decisive, however, is the second factor, that of human freedom. For it is not only *in* man that the movement of evolution is now carried on, but *by* man. It is man who invents and discovers and who has, by taking into his own hands the direction of the world, gradually replaced nature in the progress of life. Upon man, therefore, falls the awful responsibility for his future on earth. In the great game being played, says Teilhard, "we are the players as well as being the cards and the stakes. Nothing can go on if we leave the table. Neither can any power force us to remain. Is the game worth the candle, or are we simply its dupes? The question has hardly been formulated as yet in man's heart, accustomed for hundreds of centuries to toe the line; it is a question, however, whose mere murmur, already audible, infallibly predicts future rumblings. The last century witnessed the first systematic strikes in industry; the next will surely not pass without the threat of strikes in the noosphere. . . . If progress is a myth, that is to say, if faced with the work involved, we can say, 'What's the good of it all?' [then] the whole of evolution will come to a halt—*because we are* evolution." [13]

It is of the very essence of Teilhard's analysis, therefore, that in and through man evolution has not only become conscious of itself but also free to dispose of itself—it can give itself or refuse itself. "In no way does it follow from the position taken up here," he writes in *The Phenomenon of Man*, "that the success of hominiza-tion is necessary, inevitable, and certain." There is indeed "the possibility of seeing with certainty certain precise directions of the future," but only, he adds with emphasis, "*if all goes well*." . . . "We hold it [evolution] in our hands, responsible to its future for its past." Tangential energy must indeed continue its inevitable technical progress, but the forces of radial energy are subject to no such inevitability. Whether or not radial energy continues to advance toward higher consciousness depends upon

---

[13] *Ibid.*, 255, 257. (Eng. trans., 230–231, 233.)

the free decisions of men, and "each individual," says Teilhard, "can repudiate the task of ascending higher toward union." [14] Consequently what the present generation needs most is some assurance about the future of evolution. The universe has always been in motion and at this moment continues to be in motion. But will it be in motion tomorrow? "Tomorrow?" asks Teilhard. "But who can guarantee us a tomorrow anyway? And without assurance that this tomorrow exists, can we really go on living, we to whom has been given—perhaps for the first time in the whole history of the universe—the terrible gift of foresight? . . . What disconcerts the modern world at its roots is not being sure, and not seeing how it ever could be sure, that there is an outcome—*the right outcome*—to this evolution." [15]

There is an important qualification, however. The guarantee of such a right outcome must be given in the context of human freedom; it cannot come from an order imposed by coercion or sustained by fear. In Teilhard's mind this is precisely the reason for the world's present discouragement with the whole human aspiration toward unity. Up to now every gigantic effort to reduce the multitude of mankind to some order seems to have ended by stifling the human person. Communism, nazism, fascism have produced the most ghastly fetters; men hoped for brotherhood and found only ant hills. "Instead of the upsurge of consciousness which we expected, it is mechanization that seems to emerge inevitably from totalization." Yet what men forget is that, monstrous though it is, modern totalitarianism is really a distortion of something magnificent, and thus quite near the truth. When an energy runs amok, the engineer, far from questioning the power itself, simply works out his calculations afresh to see how it can be better brought under control. And in our modern world what has gone wrong is that we have neglected those forces of freedom which emerge from the depths of the human person and therefore con-

[14] *Ibid.*, 342, 25, 306. (Eng. trans., 307–308, 226, 275.)
[15] *Ibid.*, 254. (Eng. trans., 229–230.) Italics are in the French text.

stitute a unitive force which is interior, a force based not upon coercion or fear but upon love.[16]

Love is the only energy in the world that is capable of personalizing by totalizing. It alone unites human beings in such a way as to complete and fulfill them, for it alone joins them to what is deepest in themselves. This is a fact of daily experience, not only in the sexual love between man and wife, but also in the love of parents for children, the love between friends, and even to a certain extent love of one's country. In order, therefore, for men to continue in freedom toward that unity in the noosphere which is their destiny, their power of loving must gradually develop until it is capable of embracing the whole of mankind and the whole of the earth. In other words, what Teilhard has called "planetization" (intensification of the noosphere's psychic temperature from man's tighter contraction around the surface of the earth) must eventually become an "amorization." A common objection against such an idea is that beyond the radius of a select few man's capacity to love does not carry, that to love all is contradictory, a false gesture which will lead in the end to loving no one. "To this I would answer," says Teilhard, "that if, as you claim, a universal love is impossible, how can we account for that irresistible instinct in our hearts which leads us toward unity whenever and in whatever direction our deepest emotions are stirred? A sense of the universe, a sense of the whole . . . cosmic affinity and hence cosmic direction. A universal love is not only psychologically possible, it is the only complete and final way in which we are able to love." [17] At this level, then, the law of complexity consciousness has been transformed into a law of growing amorization.

But how, then, are we to explain the appearance all around us of growing repulsion and hatred? If such a strong potency is really besieging us from within and urging us to unite, what prevents it from passing into act? One thing only: "that we should overcome

---

[16] *Ibid.*, 285. (Eng. trans., 257.)
[17] *Ibid.*, 295–296. (Eng. trans., 266–267.)

the 'anti-personalist' complex which paralyzes us, and make up our minds to accept the possibility, indeed the reality, of some *source* of love and *object* of love at the summit of the world above our heads. As long as it absorbs or appears to absorb the person, the collectivity kills the love that is trying to come to birth." Unless the modern impetus toward union is leading us toward *Someone*, it must certainly end up by plunging us back into matter. In order to turn this failure that threatens us into success, what we must do is to recognize, says Teilhard, "not only some vague future existence, but also, as I must stress, the radiation *as a present reality* of that mysterious Center of our centers I have called Omega." [18]

This sudden change in the mode of conceiving Omega is indicated also in the last of Teilhard's Sorbonne lectures for 1949. "Under pain of being unable to act as keystone of the vault for the noosphere, 'Omega' can only be conceived as the *point of encounter* between the universe, once it has reached the limits of concentration, and another Center deeper still—one which is self-subsistent, an absolutely ultimate principle of irreversibility and personalization: the only *real* Omega." [19] We have here perhaps the clearest expression of Teilhard's distinction between the term "Omega" as applied to a state of collective reflection at the end of the evolutionary process, and the same term as applied to the supreme personal Being here and now responsible for the process itself. A hypothesis, therefore, of *actual* convergence would demand that the ultimate terminus of evolution be already in existence, and especially that it be personal, "loving and lovable at this very moment." Love energy, the only force capable of moving free men toward unity, must have something to draw it. "Love dies with contact with the impersonal and the anonymous. With equal infallibility it becomes impoverished with remoteness in space—and still more, much more, with remoteness in time. For

[18] *Ibid.*, 297–298. (Eng. trans., 267–268.)
[19] *Le Groupe zoologique humain*, 1949 (Paris, 1956), 162. Emphasis added to "real."

love to be possible there must be coexistence . . . a real and present noosphere goes with a real and present Center," whose influence is alone able to conquer the forces of repulsion and hatred, and so motivate sufficiently large numbers of men toward growth in spirit.[20]

Sufficiently large numbers, but not necessarily all. The future of the noosphere hinges for Teilhard upon the growth of amorization, that is, on the free circulation of love energy over the surface of the earth; for love is the highest form of that radial energy upon which true evolutionary progress depends. While it is not out of the question that "some sort of unanimity will reign over the entire mass of the noosphere" and that "hatred and internecine struggles will have disappeared in the ever warmer radiance of Omega . . . there is another possibility." [21] This other possibility is that a whole segment of humanity will reject Omega. Teilhard never loses sight of the fact that "the right outcome" of evolution is one thing, while that of the individual quite another. Ultimate victory for humanity through union with Omega does not mean personal victory for each member of humanity. The progress of radial energy could well become a stumbling block for many, since such progress means a growth of consciousness and consequently a growth of tension in the free decisions of men. It is precisely because Teilhard saw clearly that the growth of evolution meant the growth of personal responsibility that he could envision the partial failure of the whole human enterprise.

Consider, for example, the following extraordinary text, which is perhaps Teilhard's clearest statement on the ambiguity of progress for the totality of the human race:

Obeying a law from which nothing in the past has yet been exempt, evil may go on growing alongside good, and in the end it too attain its paroxysm in some specifically new form. . . . Refusal or acceptance of Omega? A conflict may spring up. In that case the noosphere,

[20] PH, 299–300. (Eng. trans., 269–270.)
[21] Ibid., 321. (Eng. trans., 288.)

in the course of and by virtue of the process which draws it together would, once it has reached its point of unification, split into two zones each attracted to an opposite pole of adoration. . . . Universal love would give life to and finally detach only a fraction of the noosphere in order to bring it to fulfillment—the part which decided to "cross the threshold," to go outside itself and into the Other. . . . [There would be] an internal schism of consciousness, ever increasingly divided on two opposite ideals of evolution, and a positive attraction by the Center of centers upon the hearts of those who turn toward it. . . .

A split [would take place] in the noosphere, divided on the form to be given to its unity; and simultaneously, endowing the event with its whole significance and value, a liberation of that percentage of the universe which, across time, space, and evil, will have succeeded in laboriously synthesizing itself to the very end. There is not to be indefinite progress, which is an hypothesis contrary to the convergent nature of noogenesis, but an ecstasy transcending the dimensions and the framework of the visible universe. Ecstasy in concord or discord; but in either case by excess of interior tension: the only biological outcome proper to or conceivable for the phenomenon of man.[22]

The evil spoken of in this passage is obviously moral evil, and its essence for Teilhard consists in the free rejection of Omega. More accurately moral evil is a refusal to *love* Omega, a refusal of that "fundamental energy of life," as Teilhard calls it, "the very blood stream of spiritual evolution." Love in Teilhard's mind is the key to the whole moral order, since it is "that psycho-moral energy" which alone can "physically build up the universe" and so bring man to his final end.[23] Its deliberate rejection, therefore, is a true injury to one's own person and to humanity as a whole, and consequently a turning away from ultimate "happiness of growth, happiness of love, and happiness of adoration."[24] The object of such love and adoration is, of course Omega. In no sense, therefore, can the *real*

[22] *Ibid.*, 321–323. (Eng. trans., 288–290.)

[23] *La Grande option*, 1939, *Oeuvres*, V (Paris, 1959), 75; *L'Esprit de la terre*, 1931, *Oeuvres*, VI (Paris, 1962), 42; *Esquisse d'un univers personnel*, 1936, *Oeuvres*, VI, 90.

[24] *Reflections sur le bonheur*, 1943, *Cahiers*, II (Paris, 1960), 64.

Omega be the final product of natural evolution. "To satisfy the ultimate requirements of our action, Omega must be independent of the collapse of forces with which evolution is woven. . . . While being the last term of its [evolution's] series, it is also *outside all series*. . . . If by its very nature it did not escape from time and space which it gathers together, it would not be Omega." [25] While by its action Omega influences directly the movement of each element in the noosphere, its own nature must be truly transcendent, capable of being present at the beginning as well as at the end of the evolutionary process.

There now follows a conclusion which represents Teilhard's final understanding of cosmic evolution. It is summarized in the terse expression, "Everything holds together from above." [26] "Contrary to appearances still accepted by physics, the great stability is not at the bottom in the infraelementary sphere, but at the top in the ultra-synthetic sphere. It is thus solely by its tangential envelope that the world goes on dissipating itself in a chance way into matter. By its radial nucleus it finds its shape and its natural consistency in gravitating against the tide of probability toward a divine focus of spirit which draws it onward." [27] The entire ascent toward life, that of life toward spirit and of spirit toward Omega, this whole movement is due not to some mechanical thrust from below, but to an *attraction* from above. It is "an inverse form of gravitation." [28]

For Teilhard, therefore, what evolution ultimately depends upon is the omnipotence of a divine and personal Omega impinging with reverence and respect upon the delicate mechanisms of human freedom and human love. At the end of his phenomenological analysis he discovered a pattern of complexity consciousness in the

[25] *PH*, 301. (Eng. trans., 270–271.)
[26] *Mon univers*, 1924, 16. The same words (*tout tient par en haut*) are used at the beginning and end of *PH*, 37 and 301. (Eng. trans., 43 and 271, but without the same terseness.)
[27] *Ibid.*, 301. (Eng. trans., 271.)
[28] *Comment je vois*, 1958, 14.

universe whose outcome was so problematical that it could provide
no guarantee whatsoever to assuage the anxiety of modern man.
The physical axis of organic evolution had now passed from the
realm of brute nature into the realm of the human person, but on
the strict level of phenomena there was no way of knowing whether
this process would continue, whether humanity would actually arrive at that point where it would be supremely one and supremely
personal. Hence there follows the second level of Teilhard's
thought, that of his "psychological act of faith," his philosophic option. This is based on the conviction that true evolutionary progress
resides not in the forces of tangential energy, now moving inevitably toward an ever greater technical mastery of mind over matter,
but rather in the forces of radial energy, which in man have become
psychosocial, urging him forward toward a fuller exercise of his
power to love. Because man today has suddenly become conscious
of what is taking place in him, the successful outcome of evolution
will now depend upon his free decision to cooperate with these
natural forces of radial energy. More concretely this means his acceptance of Omega, divine, personal, transcendent, "loving and
lovable at this very moment," who began the whole evolutionary
process, and whose powerful attraction is alone able not only to
motivate man's free decision by giving certitude of eventual success, but also to conquer man's native tendency toward repulsion
and isolation.

Consequently there is a double freedom at work in shaping
man's future on earth, that of man himself and that of God. It is
God who guarantees that the evolutionary process will continue its
converging movement toward that Center which is Himself, since
it is He who is the ultimate guarantee of the presence of love in the
noosphere. Yet it is individual man who must decide whether or
not to accept this love. There is thus a double risk involved, the risk
which God has taken in giving to man the mysterious capacity
somehow to make his own history, and the risk which each man
must take in deciding whether his own contribution to ultimate

unity in the noosphere is to be one which stifles the human person or which frees him to develop through union with others. Are we to have brotherhood or ant hills? A brave new world of human robots or ever higher forms of interpersonal communion? A collectivity of consciousness which personalizes or one which dehumanizes? No one was more aware than Teilhard de Chardin of the full dimensions of these alternatives. "It would be a complete misunderstanding of the vision which is here proposed," he writes at the end of *The Phenomenon of Man,* "to see it as a sort of human idyll instead of the cosmic drama which I have in reality wished to describe." And very early in his life he reached this conclusion: "Essentially progress is a force and the most dangerous of forces. . . . Progress is directed toward fostering in the human will reflective action and fully human choice." [29]

---

[29] *PH,* 345. (Eng. trans., 311); *Note sur le progrès,* 1920, *Oeuvres,* V, 31, 33.

Freedom, Creativity, and Scientific Discovery

Ernan McMullin

Is the question of the role of creativity in scientific discovery one of freedom at all? Creativity is not the same as freedom by any means. When someone performs a free act, when he freely chooses to spend his evening watching TV instead of helping his children with their homework, for instance, we do not think of this as being "creative." It is obvious that the vast majority of our free actions would not be regarded as "creative" in the ordinary sense of that term. Might it be, nevertheless, that all truly creative actions are free? One is tempted to reply: yes. Yet what of the poet who is seized by an almost frenzied vision and writes like a man possessed until he has conveyed it in words as best he can? When one thinks of a Coleridge, feverishly writing until his vision is interrupted, never to return, one surely thinks in terms of compulsion rather than freedom.

Is the poet free as he writes? Is the painter free as he translates his vision into color? Freedom is the most treasured attribute of man, of modern man at least, and thus to say that artistic making is not free would seem to diminish art as a truly human activity. On the other hand, to say that the artist is at all times free as he works would seem to disregard the "divine frenzy," the commanding vision, that seems at times to mark off the artist from other mortals and makes him bend everything, his materials, his friends, his own life, to the service of that relentless *daimon*.

1. *The Meaning of Freedom*

The difficulty here comes from the notorious ambiguity of the word *freedom*. I have often thought that a great deal of puzzlement could be saved were we to invent several different words here instead of, miserlike, trying to make do with one. Mortimer Adler in his magistral work on this topic some years back distinguished between three main senses in which the word *freedom* has been used.[1] The commonest usage among recent English-speaking philosophers is to make freedom equivalent to individual self-realization. In this view, a man is "free" if he is able to accomplish what he sees as best for himself. A necessary condition for such achievement is an absence of external constraining factors. But an absence of such factors is not enough, of itself, to make an act free. It must, in addition, be performed in response to the individual's own desire; he is realizing the goals he had set himself. He is acting for the good, as he sees it, but the "good" is here taken to be identical with the object of individual desire. This definition is characteristic of Hobbes, Hume, Burke, Stevenson, to name some of its best-known representatives.

The second sense in which freedom has been taken is a rather older one. From Plato onward freedom has very often been represented as something to be *acquired* by man in terms of self-control and pursuit of the good, seen here as that which is objectively good in itself. Adler calls this the "freedom of self-perfection," and notes that it dominated Greek and Roman ethics. The contrast between these two senses is very striking. The first can be impeded by external circumstance; the second cannot. Seneca notes that a slave can still be a truly "free" man, since the mind, "the better part of him is exempt . . . [and] is its own master"; only the body "can be delivered into bondage." [2] Those who speak of freedom as

---

[1] *Idea of Freedom*, New York, 1958, pp. xxvii, 689.
[2] *Moral Essays*. Translation by J. W. Basore. Cambridge (Mass.), 1935, vol. 3, p. 155. Quoted by Adler, *op. cit.*, p. 253.

self-perfection will agree that such perfection is measured by absolute and objective standards, to which everyone must measure up. A man is thus most "free" when he does what he ought. Whereas for those who equate freedom with self-realization, when a man does what he ought, he is unfree; he is under some coercion coming from outside, unless what he ought also happens to be what he desires. Furthermore, those who take freedom as self-perfection will represent man in some dualist way; there is a source of imperfection within him which has to be overcome. There is a conflict between the higher self, seeking perfection, and a lower nature, which works against it. Plato will match soul against body, and seek perfection in the overcoming of body; Freud in a not-altogether dissimilar way will match ego against id and see psychological harmony in the overcoming of the id. For those who regard freedom as self-realization, on the other hand, no such dualism or conflict is relevant. The self for them is an undivided individual; if he can attain what he desires, he is free, whether what he desires is conducive to his ultimate peace of mind or not.

The contrast between these two concepts of freedom is so marked that an act which is free in one of the senses will usually be unfree in the other. Aristotle condemns the "false idea of freedom" that would make it "doing what one wishes" [3]; in general, defenders of the concept of self-perfection will regard the liberty of self-realization rather as license, while those who prefer the latter concept of freedom will hold that the self-perfection ideal diminishes "true" freedom by imposing an unauthentic external norm.

The third type of freedom has traditionally been called "freedom of choice." Adler prefers to call it the "freedom of self-determination" because he wishes to stress the influence of repeated exercise of the freedom of choice upon the self. It is by constantly exercising one's freedom of choice in favor of the objective good, the "ought," that the freedom of self-perfection may be attained, according to most of those who speak of both, although

---

[3] *Politics*, Bk. 5, chap. 9

there are some few who deny freedom of choice and yet wish to maintain some degree of freedom of self-perfection. Freedom of choice lies in a power man possesses, usually called will, whereby in choosing one among alternatives he is not caused to do so by other antecedent causes. The act of this power is the uncaused cause of whatever concrete decision flows from it; it is not activated by other causes at its own level. To be free in this sense means to have the power to choose between alternatives without being necessitated in any way to do so. The free act here is the act of the will rather than the act of the person as a whole, which is its effect, and which will usually be externally manifested. In this the third idea of freedom differs from both the others. It is also natural to man; it does not have to be built up; nor can it be destroyed (although its issue may be affected) by external constraints. It is intrinsically unpredictable, because un-necessitated. If X can produce other effects than Y, the action of X taken alone is non-necessitating, and no analysis of it will allow us to predict Y with certainty. This is the sense of "freedom" which is ordinarily intended when someone speaks of "free choice," while in ordinary usage a "free act" will either be one which is the product of free choice, or else will be "free" in the sense of self-realization.

To use the term in one or other of the senses above does not, of course, commit one to a particular *theory* of freedom. It is only when one affirms or denies the *existence* of human freedom in one of these senses, or ranks one of them as more "basic" than another, that one has a theory of freedom, properly speaking. Christian writers, for instance, will usually maintain the existence of freedom in the second and third senses; some of them—Aquinas and Maritain among others—will defend all three. Others, like Weiss and Sartre, will concede only the third, whereas Freud will allow the other two but deny the third. When a philosopher says of one of these senses that it is not "true" freedom—Plato of the first or Sartre of the second, for example—he is implicitly assuming that freedom (whatever else it may be) is an attribute central to the understanding of man, and he is holding that the usage he criticizes overlooks this.

Let us look now at creative making and ask whether it is a "free" human activity in the light of what I have just said. Some have argued that it exhibits a kind of freedom which is peculiar to itself.[4] But it seems possible to safeguard the uniqueness of the creative moment, whether in art or in science, without having to manufacture yet another sense of that sorely tried term, "freedom." Adler suggests that it is the freedom of self-perfection that is most in evidence in the "release afforded by art." [5] Yet is this really so? It is true that the artist works furiously to get something out of his system, as it were, and that he rests in a sort of catharsis of spirit once his vision has been successfully incarnated. But there is little here of the kind of interior struggle that we have seen to be associated with the freedom of self-perfection, a struggle against a "lower self," where the object is the taming of passion and the death of all desire other than the calm desire of the Absolute. The conflict that often accompanies the poetic act seems of a very different sort; the bringing to birth of the maker's vision involves an ascent from darkness to light, an imposition of an envisioned form upon a matter exterior to the artist rather than upon the artist himself. The freedom of self-perfection finds its *raison d'être* in the person who achieves liberty of the spirit; the activity of the creator finds its *raison d'être* ultimately not in what it does for the creator but in the quality imparted to the creation.

What about the freedom of self-realization, then? This would seem to be more appropriate for the creative maker. Creative activity is dependent upon external conditions; the artist and the scientist can easily be constrained if their materials or their laboratories are taken away from them. The artist is vulnerable because he needs material to encapsulate his vision, be it only pen and paper; the scientist is vulnerable because of the tremendous organi-

---

[4] See, e.g., Daniel Christoff, *Recherche de la liberté*, Paris, 1957.
[5] *Op. cit.*, p. 590.

zation of material that must precede and support his symbolic formulations. Second, the creative mind follows its *own* bent as it strives toward expression. The artist's touchstone is his *own* image: he must be faithful to his own light rather than struggle toward some generally agreed standard of beauty. When he successfully realizes his desire in word or in color, he can be said to have acted "freely" with the freedom of self-realization.

But what of the scientist? He seems to part company with the poet at this point. His quest is governed by a criterion of verification over which he has relatively little personal control. The theoretical structure of explanation that he offers will be judged first by its success in enveloping the stubborn ground of observational facts over against him. And the criteria for success are relatively public ones, established by careful centuries of probing and formulating. Scientific inquiry, taken in its ensemble as one kind of human activity, can, it would seem, scarcely be described as free in the sense of self-realization.

2. *Freedom and "Personal Knowledge"*
in Scientific Discovery

Michael Polanyi has recently registered a vigorous disagreement with this, the conventional, view of scientific activity as the following of a specifiable set of procedures in which the personality of the individual scientist is (or at least ought to be) altogether transparent. He argues that scientific discovery is the acquisition of a "personal knowledge"; his thesis can be put in our terms by saying that the work of the scientist is at least partly "free." He marshals a great many arguments in his support; two of them deserve special mention. The procedures of science cannot be verbally specified in such a way that someone could learn how to "do" science by reading about them. Scientific work involves a period of training in which the beginner, by watching what others do, acquires a *skill*, a way of seeing and evaluating. He learns where to look for clues, and to discriminate between facts that are significant and those that are not. He sees how smooth curves are fitted to discontinuous observations, and he soon notices how expectation governs what is found. When controversies arise, he hears words like "simplicity" and "elegance" being used to justify the adoption of one theory rather than another, but he comes to defend one or the other theory himself not by finding agreed definitions for these terms but rather by simply *seeing* which theory is better.

Polanyi has effectively reminded us of something too often forgotten or denied: the presence of *controversy* in science. By focusing on older settled areas, theorists of science have been able to present the work of the scientist as an intersubjective neutral undertaking, where agreement can easily be reached on verification and criteria and the rest. If controversy is alluded to, it is treated as a temporary and regrettable state of affairs, presumably owing to one "side's" not having properly grasped the rules of the game. The suggestion is that if science were properly carried out, no controversy would ever occur. That this is an altogether naïve oversimplification does not take long to see. There is first a question of fact: all the major advances in natural science have been accompanied in their early stages by controversy. It is only in retrospect that the grounds for them and the precise way of relating evidence and theory come to be agreed upon. This stage takes considerable time, as recent controversies about the precise structure of evidence underlying the Special Theory of Relativity make clear.

Controversy is, therefore, at the heart of scientific discovery. It is only in areas already occupied, where mopping-up operations continue, that discovery can seem an objective, rule-bound affair. The reasons for this ought now to be clear. The criteria involved in decision between theories are implicit and complex; they demand on occasion something very like an aesthetic judgment. In such a judgment, the scientist participates as a person. He has his *own* vision of the universe, one that has been proved by a multitude of half-forgotten personal encounters with the physical realm in which he lives. He has been influenced by certain teachers, impressed by certain theories, motivated by certain goals. All of these myriad influences flow together in that deep-channeled activity called scientific research. There is an ineradicably personal basis in judgments that are not simple extensions of accepted rules of method.

But as time goes on and scientific methods are better and better understood, ought not such occasions of personal decision become progressively rarer? This is often assumed to be the case, yet are we in fact justified in supposing that major controversies will be rarer in science in a hundred years' time than they are today? Surely this is to forget that the criteria of science are not prior to science; our grasp of them progresses as theory progresses. Scientific method is not a sort of "given," a fully-formed tool ready for use when the occasion presents itself. It is dependent upon theory in a very intimate way. If one were to look back upon the three centuries that separate us from Galileo, it would be more meaningful to try to infer what scientific method is from the succession of theories that have gradually come to be accepted as science than to say which of those theories qualifies as science in terms of some *a priori* statement of method. In short, since method can be abstracted only by examining theories already accepted as successful, and since theory continues to develop, there is no reason to suppose that there will sometime in the future be a novel and decisive methodological instrument available for the prevention of controversy.

To see this in a more concrete way one need only look at any fundamental theoretical advance in twentieth-century physics. When Bohr introduced the notion of "quantum jumps" as a way of bringing order to the vast mass of spectroscopic data then available, his suggestion made absolutely no sense in terms of the classical electromagnetic picture. How *could* electrons jump from place to place without occupying the intervening space? The new view did not appear as an *explanation*, unless one were willing to revise one's view of what counted as "explanation." When Schwinger more recently used the idea of a "virtual transition" and of a process involving time reversal, the same question arose. If it were simply a matter of asking whether the new model takes account of all the facts, as the positivists of long ago optimistically suggested, there would be no problem here. But, in fact, there is a problem, a controversy, in this latter case one that still continues. The question is: ought virtual transitions and time reversals be allowed in a physical theory? Are they legitimate explanatory notions? If they are not, they will ultimately prove unfruitful and incoherent; but in the meantime what criteria are we to use for assessing them?

It is not merely that theories of matter have drastically changed between Maxwell's day and ours. Far more fundamental has been the change in what counts *as* a theory, in the directions in which new intelligibilities are sought. It is here that the "personal" dimension of scientific inquiry must be taken into account if we are not to fall into naïve, *post hoc* oversimplification. Does this mean that I am challenging the cherished "objectivity" of science? Of course not. My point is that objectivity can only be attained painfully and in retrospect. We can be objective today about Newtonian mechanics or about the kinetic theory of gases. We can expound them with ease and show exactly how and why they are warranted. But this is *dead* science, science already fossilized and packed away. When these theories were first put forward, not only was there no such unanimity, but, more fundamentally, there was at the time no agreed way of *achieving* unanimity on these particular issues. The gradual establishing of these theories meant the simultaneous establishing and clarification of the modes of explanation underlying them.

Presumably in times to come physicists will decide which of the two incompatible styles of doing quantum physics now in vogue, the orthodox indeterminism of Copenhagen or the heterodox determinism of Paris and Moscow, is in fact the better one. Does this mean that there is a method available *today* for adjudicating between the two, or that we only await the devising and carrying through of some crucial experiment which will exclude one of them? Whoever thinks this has very little appreciation of the issues involved in this bitter controversy, one that has divided the most advanced area of the most advanced science for almost forty years. Controversy is a central part of the *life* of science, not a temporary and embarassing side issue. And controversy leaves room for, indeed demands, a passionate adherence to a particular vision that is not shared and that at the beginning one has no way of enforcing. Such adherence is a free act on the part of the scientist; it is upon such free acts that the progress of science depends.

The freedom here in question comes closest to freedom of self-realization. It is not altogether unlike the freedom that a man exercises in the pursuit of *any* vocation, whether it be that of science, of medicine, or of road building. It is true that a vocation such as these imposes outside norms upon freedom. The imperative here comes from outside as well as from inside, reminding us of the objective norm we saw to be characteristic of the freedom of self-perfection. But the knowledge of the scientist is not self-knowledge; the research he does may have little or no impact upon him as a man. Socrates, we recall, refused to allow this possibility: his view was that all knowledge which could properly count as "science" had to lead somehow to the Good. "Scientific research," in his sense of the phrase, could not but lead to virtue, and indeed was an indispensable means of attaining it. There are still some, like Teilhard, for whom research and adoration are close together, but it would be unrealistic to suppose that the vast accelerating movement of research in all branches of the sciences today is bringing about a greater liberty of spirit than our less scientific ancestors knew.

3. *Creativity*

So far I have been considering research as though it were a single activity. I now wish to single out one aspect of it: *discovery*, and ask in what sense, if any, scientific discovery is *creative*. This is not quite the same as asking whether it is *free*. To create something is to assume entire responsibility for its coming-to-be. Only God creates in the strict sense, since all other causes depend on Him in some way, and thus their responsibility for their effects is not a total one. Every free act is an exercise of creative initiative, broadly speaking. Philosophers have always assumed that freedom of choice and the freedom of self-perfection have a creative aspect.

A. E. Taylor notes:

On the face of it, every fresh act of choice seems to be something akin to a new "creation," and it does not really add anything to the explanation of its newness to suggest that it is a manifestation of something which was there all the time but "latent."[6]

The emphasis here is partly on the *dependence* of the free act upon man, its creator, and partly on the way it makes each man what he is. Marcel calls a free act a "sort of creation of myself by myself."[7] In this sense of the term, scientific activity as a whole is "creative," since we already have seen that it is in a special way free.

It will, however, be more helpful to take "creative" in the narrower sense it has come to have in English usage. To say of a person that he is "creative" means two things: first, that what he does is original; second, that he is productive. A "creative" piece of work is an original one, one that does not follow accepted patterns. If it is truly creative, it is not just different; if that were all it took, anyone could be creative. It must also be worth while; it must set a new standard. There is a paradox here, for the creative work has to ignore previous norms and maxims to some extent, yet its value must be gauged, in part, at least, by their aid. A creative innovation, no matter how fundamental, cannot bring with it entirely new criteria of evaluation. There must be *some* continuity between old and new, not merely in terms of matter but in terms of form. Only

[6] "The Freedom of Man" in *Contemporary British philosophy*, second series, New York, 1954, p. 293. Cited by Adler, *op. cit.*, p. 425.
[7] *The Mystery of Being*, Chicago, 1951, p. 117.

where there is creation *ex nihilo* can the standards of form set by a tradition be dispensed with. God is the only Creator who does not have to worry about His predecessors. Every other creator not only finds his material already given, but also receives the germ of his vision from those who have gone before him. Before the human creator can begin to be a creator, he must first grasp the accepted norms of excellence governing the domain in which he has chosen to work. Then, and only then, can he go on to construct something which on the one hand satisfies these norms (or norms in recognizable continuity with them) and on the other hand reveals something *new*, something that is not a simple prolongation of what went before. This tension between continuity and discontinuity is at the heart of human creativity.

Continuity with a tradition, with a norm, does not, then, diminish human creativity; on the contrary, creativity requires some such support. A totally original work, one that would be outside all traditions, would not be creative in the human sense at all. To be creative is to utilize what others have at their disposal but to transcend what others have achieved by its means. It is a radically individual personal ability to go beyond the rules, to follow a light that is inward rather than outward.

When I struggle to find exactly the right word in a piece I am writing and eventually come up triumphantly with the word I wanted, this is a creative achievement because it is not governed by rule; it is a personal response admitting of degrees of success and originality. Much of our use of language is hackneyed and unreflective; word and situation correspond almost according to the stimulus-response pattern of animal behavior. But when we try to describe or evoke in our own words, when we grope along unfamiliar pathways in the effort to construct a meaning, no rules will tell us how to proceed. Rules will only help us know when we have arrived at our goal. As I search for the word I want, I cannot summon up any agreed rules of procedure. It will depend on the richness of my vocabulary, on my own native inventiveness and creative quality of mind. But when I have found the word, then I can use rules to estimate whether I am successful or not. The poet may not work by rule, but the literary critic must.

4. *Scientific Discovery*

Can this notion of creativity be applied to scientific discovery? Plato believed that creative discovery is at the heart of science, indeed that science cannot be learned, strictly speaking. It must, he thought, be appropriated by each individual by means of a series of such discoveries, each "creative," not guided by a prior explicit rule. For him, discovery, not proof, was the central moment of science. The power of scientific discovery lies within every man, slave or free, and it is this power more than any other that sets off the human soul as a thing apart, almost divine. In the *Phaedo*, Socrates falls back upon our impressive ability to recognize novel scientific truths, when endeavoring to prove to his doubting friends, Cebes and Simmias, that the soul is immortal. It seemed so remarkable to him that our minds could discover such permanence, despite the flux with which we are surrounded, that he tended to think it more likely that we are really *recollecting* knowledge, in some sense already there, rather than *discovering* it for the first time. In his later dialogues, Plato moved away somewhat from this extreme view, which would in one sense deny the possibility of scientific discovery entirely, while at the same time asserting the necessity for creative discovery—or perhaps better *recovery*—for each individual.

At the other end of the scale we might put one of Plato's own admirers, Francis Bacon, who more explicitly than anyone else in the entire history of thought maintained that creativity in science is a temporary expedient, necessary only until the rules for discovery have been found. Scientists have been forced to be creative, to improvise; the more original among them have been the better scientists. But this state of affairs, Bacon felt, is a deplorable one, and in his *Novum Organum* he set out to give a new logic of scientific discovery that he hoped would remedy it.

In the Preface he claims to

lay out a new and certain path for the mind to proceed in, starting directly from the simple sensuous perception . . . the entire work of the understanding [must] be commenced afresh, and the mind itself from the very outset not left to take its own course but guided at every step; and the business be done as if by machinery.

In Aphorism 61 of Book One he elaborates on this:

The course I propose for the discovery of the sciences is such as leaves but little to the acuteness and strength of wits, but places all wits and understandings nearly on a level. For as in the drawing of a straight line or perfect circle, much depends on the steadiness and practice of the hand, if it be done by aim of hand only, but if with the aid of rule or compass, little or nothing.

These two passages define what I shall call the "Baconian view" of scientific discovery, which would hold it possible to diminish and ultimately eliminate the need for individual creativity in science by supplying a set of automatically effective rules of procedure that anyone could use with a little training and average native ability. I want to show that this view is false, and just to prove that I am not following that favorite pastime of philosophers, flogging long-dead horses, let me quote from an article, "The New Baconians," in a recent issue of *Science* by Professor John Platt of the University of Chicago. The article puts forward a method of scientific inquiry that the author calls "strong inference," which

in its separate elements . . . is just the simple and old-fashioned method of inductive inference that goes back to Francis Bacon. The steps are familiar to every college student, and are practiced, off and on, by every scientist. The difference comes in their systematic application. Strong inference consists of applying the following steps to every problem in science, formally and explicitly and regularly: 1) devising alternative hypotheses; 2) devising a crucial experiment (or several of them) with alternative possible outcomes, each of which will, as nearly as possible, exclude one or more of the hypotheses; 3) carrying out the experiment so as to get a clean result. . . . It is like climbing a tree. At the first fork, we choose—or, in this case, "nature" or the experimental outcome chooses—to go to the right branch or the left; at the next fork, to go left or go right; and so on.

The metaphor of climbing a tree was not used by Bacon, but it would doubtless have pleased him. It does not take great wit, only a certain amount of perseverance, to find one's way up a tree. Platt notes that finding the hypotheses requires what he calls "intellectual invention," but he thinks that the main difficulty in getting up the tree does not lie there but rather in the stubborn adherence of people to theories in the face of contrary facts. One wonders what he would have said when Galileo praised Copernicus for ignoring the known data concerning relative planetary brightnesses, even though they told heavily against his own theory.

I am tempted to make the rest of my remarks a commentary on Platt's analysis, which has enough truth to be plausible but not enough to be correct. It might be better, however, to proceed in a more systematic way. Some further clarification of the notion of discovery is absolutely necessary at this point.

Broadly speaking, there are three "moments" in science: discovery, verification, and exposition. The internal structure and purpose of each differ, although they are constantly being confused with one another. This threefold division is found both in mathematics and in natural science. It has been one of the great misfortunes of the history of natural science that the division was assumed to have the same basic significance in both domains. The model of axiomatic geometry dominated all Greek and medieval writing on methodology, not geometry as we understand it today, but geometry as it was crystallized for two millennia by Euclid.

If one takes this as a model, discovery becomes the finding of axioms or principles. For any given domain of science, such principles will exist; once they are discovered, they will be seen to carry their own warrant. They do not need verification in any proper sense: they are *seen* to be true. From them all the subsidiary truths of the domain can be deduced. The warrant for these truths or theorems will rest in their deducibility from a set of principles, not in any test of an empirical sort. The axiomatic ordering reached in this way also serves as an ideal mode of exposition, since it follows the intrinsic order of intelligibility of the subject matter. If a student grasps the principles, he has in his hands the entire field. There is no need to put him to the trouble of following the more devious ways by which the original axioms were discovered. This is labor which, once accomplished, never needs to be repeated. Once the principles are established, the only problem is that of finding the most effective path from principles to theorems. If the principles are few in number, as they ideally should be, this should not be a major problem.

It can easily be seen that this schema has a very curious effect on our discovery-verification-exposition distinction. Discovery is broken into two. The discovery of axioms is a matter of casting around to find starting points that are conceptually necessary. It is an intuitive affair, not a part of science proper. The discovery of theorems, on the other hand, is deductive. Verification likewise breaks into two: axioms do not need verification, and theorems are verified by deducing them from axioms.

Exposition comes to dominate science because in the layout of axiom and theorem that Euclid gives one can immediately see both how every part of the system is discovered and how each is verified. Indeed, for the theorems, discovery and verification are identical: a theorem is verified by discovering, i.e., deducing it.

In this model of science creative discovery plays almost no role. The modern mathematician will point out that the locus of creativity in the mathematics he knows is not in the axiomatizing of already-defined systems, such as plane geometry, but rather in the extending and redefining of fundamental concepts, such as *number* or *curvature* or *continuum*. The proof of a complex theorem or the axiomatizing of a domain such as arithmetic may be important, but most of the real activity in mathematics lies elsewhere. If one asks what research mathematicians *do*, one is not asking about the neat fossilized systems and problems given to students to enable them to learn techniques. This is mathematics as *exposition*, the least important of the three, but the one that defined not only mathematics but the entire methodology of science for nearly two thousand years. If mathematics be what adult mathematicians do—which seems a reasonable definition, at least to begin with—then discovery and verification become the central interests of methodology, discovery as it may be inferred from the scribbled notes of the researcher, not from the finished research paper where all traces of it have been carefully concealed.

But our interest here is rather in the kind of discovery that characterizes natural science. In the two books of *Analytics*, Aristotle proposed a methodology for all science that was largely shaped by a geometrical ideal, and by an emphasis on exposition, rather than on discovery or verification. The dominant notion in it is demonstration, which is not demonstration in the ordinary sense, since he frequently gives examples of allegedly "demonstrative" syllogisms where the conclusion is obviously better warranted (i.e., better known to us) than the premises are. Thus, for instance, from the premises that the planets are near and that whatever is near does not twinkle, he deduces that planets do not twinkle and calls this a "demonstration" of the property of non-twinkling in planets.[8] But since this is the property that we know first and from which our whole analysis begins, it is clear that "demonstration" here is not equivalent to verification, but rather to "successful incorporation as conclusion in a deductive system." His famous distinction between truths that are "better known in themselves" and truths that are "better known to us" is at the root of the difficulty, and it prevented him from formulating an adequate

[8] *Posterior Analytics*, I, 13.

notion of scientific warrant. What he could not see was that the main (though perhaps not the only) warrant for the mysterious truths "better known in themselves" was not some sort of internal self-evidence but the fact that truths "better known to us" (i.e., empirical consequences) could be deduced from them. The warrant, in other words, ought to have gone from the conclusion back to premises rather than the other way around.

The ideal given in the *Posterior Analytics* inverted the order of verification proper to an empirical science, and thus obscured the notion of theoretical discovery. Aristotle notes that "every belief comes either through syllogism or from induction." [9] Since the type of induction he favored was induction by complete enumeration, discovery either way would be more or less automatic. He also spoke of induction by incomplete enumeration, what we would call generalization, as well as an induction which would somehow lead to an insight into first principles. This last was never worked out, and in any event it was overshadowed by the twofold division of scientific inferences into deductive and inductive-enumerative that he bequeathed to his successors.

When Aristotelian natural science was replaced by Galilean-Newtonian mechanics in the seventeenth century, there was at first very little change in official declarations of what a science is.[10] What Galileo and Descartes had to say on this was not very different from what Aristotle said. But what they did as scientists was very different. They made extensive use of what has more recently been called the "hypothetico-deductive," or HD, method. In his great *Dialogo*, Galileo took as a hypothesis that the moon is made of a similar substance to the earth and inferred from this a great many consequences about light reflection and so forth. The fact that all of these consequences are verified in their variety and detail he takes to be a direct warrant for the hypothesis from which

[9] *Prior Analytics*, II, 23; 68b 14.
[10] See E. McMullin, "What Makes It Science?" in *Technology and Culture*, ed. by G. McLean, Catholic University Press.

they can be derived. This is a new kind of warrant, one that Plato had hinted at rather clearly in the *Phaedo* but exactly the opposite to the warrant afforded by "demonstration" in Aristotle's *Analytics*. It is an empirical warrant, but it is qualified, corrigible, progressive. It can be either positive or negative, that is, it can either support a hypothesis or exclude one. Bacon was the first to stress the power of negative HD: "in the establishment of any true axiom, the negative instance is the more forcible of the two." [11] He has been followed in this by a whole line of theorists up to Karl Popper who stress that science progresses rather by the negating of hypotheses than by the establishing of them. Nevertheless, the continued corroboration of a hypothesis, such as that of Galileo about the moon, can legitimately be considered a process of verification.

Let us return now to our discovery–verification–exposition distinction, and see how it fares in the context of contemporary natural science. First, it is clear that the method of *verification* is the HD method predominantly. There are two qualifications to this. First, simple generalizations (such as "mosquitoes breed on the surface of water") rest upon an inductive warrant. The reason we *initially* accept them is not that they have been put forward as a hypothesis and then continually tested, but rather that we have a certain limited number of instances in direct support.

Second, and more controversially, there are grounds for supposing that part, at least, of the warrant for a physical theory may well be intrinsic to the theory itself, like its simplicity or its aesthetic beauty or a certain type of coherence. From Galileo to Einstein, practically every major theoretical scientist has confessed to using criteria of this sort, and if one wishes to defend a purely empiricist theory of science, one is either forced, like Professor Platt, to chide scientists who back their idea occasionally against the facts because of some inner quality they see in the theory itself, or else one must

[11] *Novum Organum*, aph. 46.

say that such things simply do not happen in respectable scientific circles. Neither of these alternatives seems to me an attractive one, and I am led to conclude that the HD model of verification, while sufficient to account for the gradual progression of models within such areas as molecular biology or nuclear physics, is not adequate in accounting for the degree of warrant known historically to have been attributed from the beginning to major new theories such as the heliocentric hypothesis of Copernicus or Einstein's Special Theory of Relativity, theories that were responsible for the entire reconstructing of a world view.

The method of *exposition* in natural science is predominantly deductive. Students are presented with theories and asked to work pencil-and-paper problems in terms of them. The theories are presented in a deductive, sometimes even in a semi-axiomatic, way. Experiments are used by way of classroom demonstration, not as a genuine means of verification. To perform the Newton's Rings experiment helps us to understand what the phenomenon was that Newton explained, but the textbook treatment of it gives hardly any idea of the actual historical interconnections between the original experimental findings and the various hypotheses Newton put forward to account for them.

When we come to *discovery*, the matter is much more complicated, because so many different sorts of things can be discovered in scientific work, all of them involving somewhat different methodologies.[12] I shall distinguish between four different kinds of discovery. First there in the discovery of new *facts*, like Fraunhofer's discovery of dark lines in the spectrum of sunlight. Second, there is the discovery of hitherto-unknown empirical correlations such as Boyle's Law. Third, there is the discovery of new hypotheses. Fourth, there is the discovery that these new hypotheses are in fact verified.

[12] See R. Taton: *Reason and Chance in Scientific Discovery*, New York, 1962.

5. Creativity and Scientific Discovery

Let me dispose rapidly of three of these. First, about facts. In a sense, *all* facts have to be discovered. Sometimes it takes great skill or even genius to notice a particular fact as significant for science; in these cases, discovery is a sort of *Gestalt* affair wherein only one man may see the face in the trees. It may be noted that it is almost never a matter of direct perception, so that the analogies brought by some authors from perception theory are slightly misleading. The data are ordinarily pointer readings or symbolic expressions; "seeing" the bump on the experimental curve as significant is a more intellectual sort of "seeing" than is seeing faces in a drawing of a forest. Nevertheless, it must be noted that a special sort of creativity may be involved here, a breaking through normal modes of intellectual structuring.

The discovery of new empirical laws can sometimes be described in terms of so-called inductive logic, especially if a simple generalization ("these A's are B's, so there is some probability that all A's are B's"), or a statistical correlation ("the death rate due to lung cancer among cigarette smokers is four times as high as among nonsmokers") is involved. The means of establishing these is relatively well defined and requires little creative power. More often the law will have a partially theoretical character; it will go beyond the data in a way which is more characteristic of theory than of the simple generalizations of inductive logic.

The discovery that hypotheses are verified is more properly regarded as verification than as discovery. Karl Popper has muddied the waters almost beyond remedy by naming his well-known book *The Logic of Scientific Discovery*. There is nothing about a book which gains so much permanence as its title. People who have never read the book may still be unconsciously formed by the assumptions hidden in the title. What Popper explicitly means by his title is this: the logic of scientific verification. This logic is for him the HD procedure, which is manifestly not a structure of discovery, except in the special sense in which a hypothesis "may be discovered to be a discovery," that is discovered to be properly corroborated.[13]

It is ironic that Popper by choosing this unfortunate title should help to spread the view that there is a logic of hypothesis discovery, since he is the one who perhaps more than anyone else denies that there is such a logic: "The initial stage, the act of conceiving or inventing a theory, seems to me neither to call for logical analysis nor to be susceptible of it." [14]

This brings me to the last and much the most important sense of the term, "discovery," for science, the sense just defined by Popper as "the act of conceiving or inventing a theory." It scarcely needs noting that this sort of discovery is the very nerve of scientific progress. If our method of verification is to be hypothetico-deductive, then science is going to be altogether dependent upon the supply of good hypotheses. It is here, above all, that creativity is to be found in scientific work; it is here that the difference between a great scientist and a good one counts most. We pay tribute to Einstein, for example, not so much because of his work on the verification of his theories as for the initial inspiration of genius that led him to formulate them as he did.

Theoretical discovery, as we may call it, is not always a single flash. More often there is a gradual fitting and trying, the reformulation and tightening of an old concept, such as mass, perhaps, or the introduction of a new concept, such as entropy, that only gradually comes clear. It is often associated with new models, like Bohr's model of the hydrogen atom or more recent models of the atomic nucleus or of DNA structure. It is a fact that most of the names considered the foremost in the history of science are associated with major theoretical discoveries of this sort. It is just here,

[13] *The Logic of Scientific Discovery*, London, 1959, p. 31.
[14] *Op. cit.*, p. 31.

then, that Bacon's effort to "place all wits and understandings nearly on a level" fails. His instructions approximate to an HD method of verification with an inductive method of discovery, a pattern that Mill would later work out in more detail. But he nowhere appreciates how central it is to his "machinery," as he calls it, to *find* the hypotheses he needs, and it is fairly clear that this is where the machinery breaks down and creativity re-enters.

6. *Logic and Creativity*

But perhaps someone will find a logic of theoretical discovery which will allow it to be carried on in a relatively automatic and orderly way, just as deduction or induction. Norwood Hanson in a recent series of articles has been arguing for a third method of inference, which he calls retroduction; he suggests in a rather hesitant way that this method would furnish a partial logic of theoretical discovery.[15] He concedes that a manual to help scientists make discoveries is impossible, and yet he seems to think that there is a sort of inference leading, if not to hypothesis, at least to a knowledge of the "type" that the hypothesis must belong to. It is difficult to see what he means by "type" and by "inference" here, and indeed most of his argument consists of showing that the HD model does not serve to explain discovery, which is hardly surprising since this model was proposed as an account of verification not of discovery. Since he quotes C. S. Peirce in his support, it may be easier to cast an eye at what Peirce has to say about a third type of inference, which he calls variously "retroduction," "abduction," or simply "hypothesis."[16] He defines retroduction by the following formal pattern: a fact is observed, if such-and-such a hypothesis

---

[15] "Is There a Logic of Discovery?" in *Current Issues in the Philosophy of Science*, ed. by H. Feigl and G. Maxwell, New York, 1961, pp. 20–35; "Retroductive Inference" in *Philosophy of Science*, ed. by B. Baumrin, London, 1963, pp. 21–37.

[16] *Collected Papers*, ed. by P. Weiss and C. Hartshorne, Harvard, 1931–1935; I, pp. 71–74; II, pp. 372–388; V, p. 189; VI, pp. 477, 522–528.

were true, this fact would follow; therefore this hypothesis has some likelihood. One notices the key ambiguity right away: is the retroduction the set of all three statements here or only the second? Is the retroduction simply the *discovery* of the hypothesis or is it the linking of the hypothesis with the desired consequence in a probabilistic structure? If it is the former, then no pattern has been discovered for it other than that afforded by its own definition. To say that we have discovered a hypothesis H to account for evidence E contains implicitly the claim that H implies E. So that to give "H implies E" as a pattern for retroduction in no way establishes that there is a mode of inference, in any proper sense of the term, leading from E to H.

Peirce appears to confuse a rule of inference with a formal definition. If I have a statement of the form $p \rightarrow q$ and p is true, I can infer that q is true. That is, I have sufficient grounds in the premises for supposing the conclusion to be true. But if I have a statement of the form q, and I want to derive a hypothesis of the form $p \rightarrow q$, it will not help me in the least to say that "q, $p \rightarrow q$, therefore probably p" together form a pattern defining what we mean by hypothesis. That is precisely *all* it does: it defines what I *mean* by the term "hypothesis" but it in nowise helps me to make one. In his last note on this topic Peirce himself conceded that hypothesis came by the suggestion of "instinct"; and he argued from our success in formulating hypotheses to a kind of correlation between our natural instinct and the workings of nature.[17]

It does not seem to be the case, then, that there is a logic of theoretical discovery, a set of formal rules saying that from evidence of type E we can infer hypothesis H, and from evidence of type E_2 we can infer H_2, and so on. The formulation of every hypothesis is a radically singular act. This does not mean that some resemblances might not be found. But it does mean that an *inference* from evidence to hypothesis, a process of reasoning following

[17] *Op. cit.*, VI, 477.

formal specifiable rules, is simply not possible. There is a leap involved which is nevertheless a rational one, since it is guided by experience of the field to which evidence and hypothesis alike belong. The person who has most made his own every detail of the field, of every resonance between the items in it, will be most likely to find the best hypothesis, always supposing he has to a superb degree the sheer ability to make fruitful hypotheses that has often been used to define scientific genius.

There are other ways of studying the leap of hypothesis. The historian can try to find the reasons why a particular scientist was led to suggest a particular theory. He may have the scientist's own testimony or the testimony of others who worked with him. The sociologists can ask whether social forces have any effect on the creativity of the individual scientist, and in particular whether they ever cause him to adopt one hypothesis rather than another in his scientific research. There are two different questions that the psychologist can (and does) ask: What is going on when a person makes a hypothesis? In other words, can anything be said about the structure of the creative process here? The second and somewhat less interesting question is: Can behavioral criteria be specified in terms of which scientific creativity can be attributed to individuals?

Nearly all the vast amount of writing on scientific creativity by American psychologists in recent years has been in response to the second question, not the first, since only the second is amenable to treatment in behaviorist terms. They find out which persons in science are described by some competent group of judges as "creative." Then they try to find out what other more easily measurable traits this group has in common. It is hoped that out of all this a clearer definition of "creative ability" will emerge, with some convenient, readily administered tests at hand to measure it. So far results have been quite unimpressive, but doubtless this is in part due to the difficulty as well as to the vagueness of the question. It is worth noting that the psychologists assume that the major factor in scientific success is a creative one, that creative ability is a relative constant of personality, and that it is extremely variable from one person to another.

The other question has been much less explored. Some, like Ghiselin and Koestler, have been talking recently about the sources of creative inspiration. They note the role of analogies in setting up new hypotheses, and the consequent necessity for a rich and complex grasp of the interrelations between the conceptual elements of the field of inquiry. Koestler has much to say about the part played by the unconscious as a kind of dark well in which many fishes swim that a quick heave may bring to the surface. Poincaré, in perhaps the most famous recounting and analysis of a creative act, preferred to speak of swarms of ideas whose impact and resulting combinations produced novelty.

It is obvious that psychological analyses of this sort are as yet a long way from telling us how the creative act of theory formation occurs. To "tell us how it occurs"—this sounds once again as though to explain creativity we have got to explain it away. But this is not in the least the case. A great scientist's work would not seem any the less great if we were to discover the fragmentary reasons and subconscious analogies that suggested to him an important hypothesis. What made his achievement a unique creative one was not its inability to yield *any* sort of pattern in retrospect but rather the fact that he and he alone put the reasons and the analogies together in an act of creation.

Religious Freedom

John Courtney Murray, S.J.

I might possibly discuss the general problem of religious freedom from a theoretical point of view. Perhaps, however, it will be more interesting if I deal with the issue as it has arisen and been argued at the Council. Much detail has been reported in the press. Synthesis therefore will be my chief effort.

The first great achievement of the Council was to open the subject to full and free discussion. It is a well known fact that theological dialogue on the subject had been inhibited for more than a decade, since the removal from circulation of the symposium, *Tolérance et communauté humaine.* In consequence, certain differences of opinion within the Church were never clearly brought to light and argued out. This has now been done. The Council Fathers have publicly discussed three separate schemata or draft-texts. Hundreds of pages of comment and criticism have been sent in to the Secretariat for the Promotion of Christian Unity, and in them all shades of opinion have been stated, sometimes at considerable length. In addition, a number of useful books and a larger number of articles have been published. The subject therefore has received the thorough discussion that was necessary before a conciliar statement could be made.

The first schema was submitted to the conciliar Fathers at the beginning of the second session in 1963. It formed part of the schema on ecumenism composed by the Secretariat, whose membership at the time comprised less than a dozen bishops, together with a small number of *periti*. The chapter on religious freedom was discussed only briefly and in general. And time ran out before a vote could be taken on the question of whether the text was in general acceptable as the basis of further discussion.

Between the end of the second session and the last days of January some three hundred and eighty interventions, as they are called, were sent in by the conciliar Fathers. After detailed study and analysis of these a new text was put together by the Secretariat, whose membership had now been increased to thirty bishops, the complement of a full conciliar commission. This text was no longer part of the schema on ecumenism; it assumed the form of a separate Declaration. At the outset of the third session, in 1964, it was submitted to a searching critique from every point of view in the *aula* itself. In addition, some one hundred and forty interventions were sent in to the Secretariat. The great majority of them supported the schema in principle, but there were many reservations and criticisms of detail.

In the light of this abundant critique a sub-committee of the Secretariat undertook the work of revision. It proved to be lengthy and arduous; it went through at least five major stages of change. Finally, the document was submitted to the Secretariat in several plenary sessions. The discussion was detailed and complete. At the end of it, the approval was unanimous. Moreover, as the press reported at the time, the text was also examined by a small mixed commission of bishops both from the Secretariat and from the Theological Commission. It was approved with one dissenting vote. Finally, the text was submitted to the full Theological Commission, which is the highest conciliar commission on matters of doctrine. The vote reported in the press was twenty-one in favor to six opposed.

Again the schema was not put to a vote in the *aula*. (The usual procedure is to call for a vote on the general tenor and content of a schema; if it is favorable, the Fathers submit in writing their reservations, called *modi*; these are examined by the commission that sponsored the schema, and are accepted or rejected, in each case a reason being given in writing; the revised text is then resubmitted to the conciliar Fathers, who express by vote their satisfaction or dissatisfaction with the changes made.) The failure, for the second time, to come to a vote on the Declaration on Religious Freedom was, as is well known, the occasion for an outburst of indignation in the *aula*. (Some one called it *dies irae*, the day of wrath.) It can hardly be gainsaid, however, that the decision not to call for a vote was technically correct. In order to reckon with the criticisms made, it had been necessary to prepare what was, in fact, a substantially new text which, according to the rules of the Council, should not have been put to a vote without previous discussion, for which there was no time. Moreover, in retrospect (although not at the moment), it was generally recognized that the decision to postpone a vote was wise. One could hardly say that the discussion of the subject had not been adequate. The fact was that everyone had ample opportunity to express his views, either in public or in written interventions. On the other hand, the discussion had perhaps been too rapid, on a subject that had never been argued so fully before. It may be said, in consequence, that some of the Fathers had not had time properly to digest the issues and to come to clarity in the matter.

What were the issues? They had, of course, developed in the ongoing course of history, which always tends to put new questions by altering the manner of asking old questions. The first argument, therefore, was between the older theory of religious tolerance and the more contemporary theory of religious freedom. The former theory had assumed systematic form during the post-Reformation era of the national "confessional" states, which themselves took shape, both Protestant and Catholic, chiefly after the Peace of Westphalia (1648). This theory became the received opinion in the nineteenth century in the course of the conflict between the Church and Continental laicism. Leo XIII himself accepted the theory on one level of his doctrine, on which he was concerned with the defense of the Catholic nation-state against the inroads of laicism. (On a deeper level of doctrine Leo XIII also undertook and achieved that *ressourcement*—that is, creative return to sources—which is always necessary in order to initiate vital development of the tradition.)

The theory of religious tolerance takes its start from the statement, considered to be axiomatic, that error has no rights, that only the truth has rights—and exclusive rights. From this axiom a juridical theory is deduced, which distinguishes between "thesis" and "hypothesis." The thesis asserts that Catholicism, *per se* and in principle, should be established as the one "religion of the state," since it is the one true religion. Given the institution of establishment, it follows by logical and juridical consequence that no other religion, *per se* and in principle, can be allowed public existence or action within the state (which normally, in this theory, is considered to be identical and co-extensive with society). Error has no rights. Therefore error is to be suppressed whenever and wherever possible; intolerance is the rule. Error, however, may be tolerated when tolerance is necessary by reason of circumstances, that is, when intolerance is impossible; tolerance remains the exception. Tolerance therefore is "hypothesis," a concession to a factual situation, a lesser evil.

It was to be expected that this theory would be presented to the Council, and it was. It is further to be expected that this theory will, in the end, be rejected by the Council, which has taken seriously, here as elsewhere, the issue of *aggiornamento*, in accordance with the mind of John XXIII. It was evident—and the fact has been reported—that the conciliar Fathers in general took the view that, here as elsewhere, a development of doctrine has taken place and that its term is to be accepted and affirmed as valid. This term is the affirmation of religious freedom as a human and civil right. John XXIII noted the root of the development, as well as its term, when he pointed to man's contemporary growth in the consciousness of his own dignity, both personal and civil, in consequence of which men today demand civil liberties—primary among them, religious freedom—and such due limitation of the powers of government as will guarantee and foster in society that civil freedom which is a constituent of man's dignity. Religious freedom is an exigence of human dignity. It is therefore a human right. And it requires sanction as a civil right, guaranteed by human law.

This is, in brief, the second view of the matter that was presented to the conciliar Fathers, as might again have been expected. Moreover, in this view the concept of religious freedom is altogether definite. It is understood to be an immunity, a freedom from coercion, whether legal or extralegal. Moreover, the immunity is twofold. A man may not be forcibly constrained to act against his conscience, and he may not be forcibly restrained from acting according to his conscience. Furthermore, in this view the extension of the concept is not in doubt; it is a matter of agreement not only among jurists but among theologians, both Protestant and Catholic. Religious freedom is immunity from coercion in what concerns religious worship, observance, practice, and witness—in all cases, both private and familial and also public and social.

It is one thing to agree on what religious freedom means; this agreement is today widespread. It is quite another thing to agree on the grounds for asserting that religious freedom is a human right; this agreement has not been reached so generally. In 1958, for instance, the World Council of Churches established a special study-commission on religious freedom. Its premise was the admitted fact that, while the Protestant community was universally in favor of religious freedom, there was no consensus with regard to the reasons for being in favor of it. The situation was hardly better five years later, when A. F. Carrillo de Albornoz published his useful little book, *The Basis of Religious Liberty*. It contains a competent summary and analysis of the differences of opinion among ecumenical theologians, not on the concept of religious freedom, but on the manner of making the argument for its validity. Very briefly, three questions were a matter of continuing discussion. First, what is the relation between the contemporary

technical concept of religious freedom and the evangelical notion
of Christian freedom? "For freedom," Paul writes to the Galatians,
"Christ has set us free" (Gal. 5:1). In what sense is civil freedom of
religion to be considered an exigence of Paul's "freedom"? Second,
in arguing for religious freedom, what place should be allowed for
arguments of the political and legal order? Third, how are rational
arguments and more directly Christian-theological arguments to be
combined in the full statement of the case?

It was not surprising that comparable differences of opinion
should have arisen among the conciliar Fathers within the vast
majority who stood in favor of religious freedom. It might be fair to
distinguish four general lines of thought.

First, there were those who were a bit dismayed by the theoretical complexities of the matter and therefore thought it better for
the Council to make a brief statement of a practical character,
without entering into argument. The objection to this position was
obvious. The Council would leave itself open to the old charge of
opportunism, to the oft-repeated complaint that the Church does
not support religious freedom in principle but only as a practical
solution for a practical problem. Hence this position won little
support.

Second, there were those who wished to begin the argument with
the notion of freedom of conscience. All men are called by God to
a destiny beyond this world. This divine vocation is mediated by
conscience; man therefore must be left free to follow his conscience
and thus fulfill God's will for him. In this structure of argument
the juridical notion of the free exercise of religion appears as a
conclusion or deduction from the freedom of personal interior
religious decision. Against this position a variety of objections
could be launched, and they were.

The argument—it was said—contains an inference from the
subjective order of conscience to the objective order of rights. But
this inference is valid only in the case of the conscience that is
rightly formed according to norms that are objectively true. In

contrast, the erroneous conscience has no rights. So runs the objection. To meet it, one would have to enter the whole issue of the rights of the erroneous conscience. Not only is the issue complicated; it is also irrelevant to the concrete problem of religious freedom, for the simple reason that it is neither within the power nor within the competence of government to judge whether conscience be erroneous or not, in good faith or in bad faith. This too was pointed out, but the fact leaves the theoretical argument still in the air. The argument, others therefore said, fails to reach a conclusion that is broad enough. From the necessary freedom of a man's interior religious decision it does indeed follow that a man may not be coerced into acting against his conscience. This, however, is no longer a controversial issue. It was settled, both among Protestants and among Catholics, in the post-Reformation era, as the wars of religion ran out and the folly as well as the injustice of coerced religious worship or observance became apparent. The real issue remains; it concerns man's right to freedom from restraint or impediment in acting according to his conscience. Does religious freedom in this sense follow from the freedom of conscience or even from man's duty to follow conscience? There were those who thought that it did not.

It was further objected that the methodology inherent in the argument from conscience was too abstract, deductive, unsuited to a problem in human rights. Whatever the recent direction of the so-called "moral curve" in other areas, in the area of human and civil rights it has been slowly upward. The dignity of man has always been a truth. In modern times, however, there has been a growth in consciousness of the truth and in sensitivity to its exigences—not least perhaps in consequence of the brutal insensitivities to these exigences that recent history has displayed. Therefore argument about human rights, including religious freedom, has to be informed by historical consciousness, by an awareness that demands inherent in the nature of man manifest themselves and come to recognition in history, under the impact of developing human experience. Deductive argument therefore is not enough. Good moral philosophy, like all good philosophy, must begin with man's historical experience and undertake to discern in it the intentions of human nature, the rational imperatives that rise from the depths of the concrete human person, the dictates of reason that claim affirmation as natural law.

A third line of thought therefore appeared, influenced by respect for historical consciousness, unwilling to lose sight of the heart of the matter through involvement in subtle dialectics concerning the rights of conscience. In this third line it is granted at the outset that rights may not be founded on error, but only on truth. The first immediate affirmation, however, is that rights are inherent in persons. Rights are founded on the dignity of the person, which is the first truth of the social order—the order in which rights are affirmed and exercised. The dignity of the person is a basic constituent element of the objective moral order, the order on which society itself and its laws and processes must be based. Beginning, therefore, with the dignity of the person, the argument begins in the objective order of truth and moves wholly in it.

The ensuing affirmation is that the dignity of the person requires, as *Pacem in terris* asserted, that in the conduct of his life a man should act on his own judgment, with freedom, out of an inner sense of duty, under immunity from outside pressures or coercions. The uses of freedom therefore are not to be limited unless there be a legitimate reason for their limitation. In the social order, freedom is the principle, the rule, the method. If freedom is to be limited, warrant must be shown. Such warrant does not exist antecedently or in the abstract. And it is not created by the sheer fact that a man's life or action is based on some manner of error or falsity. Before any duty and right to limit freedom can come into existence and be invoked, even by government, it must be shown that the use of freedom has resulted in some manner of serious social transgression—some violation of the rights of others, some offense against generally accepted standards of public morality, some grave disturbance of the public peace. These general principles set the line of thought of the third school. In their application to the issue of religious freedom they sharply accent the notion itself as a juridical notion whose immediate foundations are in the order of reason.

At this juncture, a fourth line of thought appears. It does not collide in contradiction to the third line. On the contrary, it presents itself as complementary. Its proponents are not content to defend religious freedom simply as a juridical notion. To do this, they say, would be to fail to pursue the matter *à fond*. (The advocates of this line are mostly French-speaking.) They wish, therefore, to radicate religious freedom in religion itself—concretely, in the Scriptures, and in the traditional doctrine of the necessary freedom of Christian faith. Moreover, they feel—perhaps a bit confusedly—that a conciliar statement on the subject should be theological in tone. It should draw primarily on the sources of faith, not be content simply with rational argument, and not assign primacy to rational argument.

It should be said here that the difference of opinion between the third and fourth lines of thought had not a little to do with the postponement of a vote on the Declaration at the third session. The difference was not so much of opinion as of perspective. But it served to confuse the issue and render judgment uncertain. In particular, it was the cause of a division within the ranks of the supporters of religious freedom. This was the more true for the reason that those who wish to "theologize" religious freedom are not themselves agreed on the way to do it.

There are those who simply "quote and argue." They quote the texts of St. Paul and the Gospels texts in which the message of salvation is presented to man for his free acceptance, and from these texts they draw conclusions. To others, however, this technique is simplistic and unconvincing. It also runs the risk of "triumphalism," which to this Council is anathema. That is, it runs the risk of presenting religious freedom as somehow a purely Christian invention, whereas every student of history knows that the idea has been developed and brought to realization also, and quite importantly, by the force of purely secular dynamisms. Therefore these others wish to make a more historical argument. The Gospel, they say, is indeed a message of liberation to man. It represents a long leap forward in God's gradual education of man to freedom—to the freedom that consists in man's submission to the "law of the Spirit which gives life" (Rom. 8:2), whereby man is freed from all worldly enslavements that are unworthy of him. This message of freedom was deposited as a leaven in the mass of history, which throughout the centuries has worked hiddenly, and far beyond the visible confines of the Christian Church herself. The slow movement of mankind to a sense of human dignity and freedom, and to institutional expressions of this sense, has been due not least to the hidden spiritual power of the Gospel's message of liberation. So, in brief, runs the argument.

Perhaps I may leave the whole subject here. I have simply undertaken to indicate the lines of thought that have crossed and completed one another in the course of the conciliar argument on religious freedom. It has been a high argument, carried on with great seriousness and complete freedom. For my part, I do not think its outcome is in doubt. None of the differences of opinion or perspective are, in the end, irreconcilable. I think the outcome will be consensus in support of religious freedom in its most solid and generous sense.

Authority and Responsibility

Robert O. Johann, S.J.

The notion of responsibility includes and presupposes the notion of freedom. One is responsible for his actions only to the extent that one is their self-determining source. We are responsible only for what we freely do. To talk about responsibility and authority, therefore, is already and inescapably to be talking about freedom and authority.

The reason, however, why I use the word responsibility rather than freedom is to highlight the special problem that confronts the person under authority. This problem is not the one that arises from the conflict between my desire to do as I please and my obligation to do as I am told. It does not arise from the idea that authority is necessarily restrictive of one's capacity for self-determination. Few persons would question the need for genuine authority if society is to be able to achieve its ends. And since the person can only thrive and flourish in society, there are few who would question the need for genuine authority if the person him-self is to achieve his own ends. The problem confronting the person under authority is not the one of reconciling spontaneity and obligation. It is much more profoundly the problem of reconciling two apparently conflicting obligations: that, first of all, of doing always and only what I myself think is right, and that, on the other hand, of doing as I am told when I am told by legitimate authority. For if I do only what I am told when I think it is right, that is, when I happen to agree with it, how can I be said to have the proper respect for legitimate authority? On the other hand, if I do

141

what I am told regardless of whether or not I think it is right, how can I be said to have the proper respect for my own integrity as a responsible person?

This, I think, is the problem of freedom and authority as most people experience it today. It is the problem of having to do what I am told when commanded by legitimate authority, and yet at the same time of being ultimately responsible for whatever I do, even when I do as I am told.

The New Sense of Responsibility

Although the tension that arises from being personally responsible for one's actions and at the same time subject to the demands of legitimate authority has always been with us, it has taken on a more intense form today. This has to do with the new sense of the person that dominates contemporary thinking. There are not a few philosophers who speak today of the crisis of the personal. They would make their own the judgment of Father Teilhard de Chardin that we have neglected in our theories and in our acts to give due place to the person and the forces of personalization. They would insist, moreover, that certain developments in the contemporary world have made it impossible to continue any longer in this neglect.

First of all there is the increased sense of time and history. Institutions and formulations that were formerly considered to be absolute are now seen to be relative, the products of history. Traditional patterns and conventions which were once thought of as presuppositions, part of the given and set up by God, are now viewed as human accomplishments. However much they may embody absolute values, they are still only limited and contingent expressions of those values and must be measured for their shortcomings against the very values they try to express. Thus ways and norms of behaving which were once beyond discussion are now considered as proper matter for discussion.

Second, there is the tremendous growth in the area of communications. The individual is no longer able to be reared in his formative years within the context of a single world view that gives him *the* truth about his place in the universe. From infancy he is bombarded by a plurality of traditions. The result has been to weaken the authority of any one of them as normative for his life. The individual himself must decide the stand he will take and do so on his own responsibility.

There has thus emerged a new sense of personal transcendence. The person is not merely a being who has emerged from the determinism of nature so that the conduct of his life is a problem placed in his own hands; he is now seen to transcend social and institutional determinisms as well. Just as in the past, to give way to a life of instinct was considered a betrayal of his very personhood, so now the same judgment is passed on any kind of life that merely accepts the order it finds without trying always to improve it.

The scope of personal responsibility has thus been immeasurably broadened. The person is no longer responsible merely for the conduct of his life and for bringing it into conformity with pre-existing patterns. He now sees himself as responsible for the very patterns themselves. For contemporary man, nothing finite and determinate is final or incapable of improvement. The person today sees himself in the role of a perpetual and wholesale renovator.

The Breakdown of Traditional Images

Man's new awareness of his creative role has contributed to his sense of the inadequacy of the older images in terms of which he tried to understand his life. He finds it difficult, for example, to see himself merely as a *being under law*: one who is called to regulate his life in terms of fixed and determinate norms. For the order of the given and the determinate is precisely what he calls into question. A being whose vocation is to be the judge and shaper of patterns cannot have his meaning simply in terms of them.

On the other hand, except in the case of some existentialists, he is reluctant to assume that he is a law unto himself. He is therefore bent at present on finding a new understanding of what it means to be under law, an understanding which is consistent with his own vocation to creativity. For he knows that until he finds a way of reconciling his creative role with his creaturely status, he will not be freed from the deep anxiety that presently plagues him.

In like manner, the image of life as a *pursuit of perfection*, conceived in terms of a fixed goal, has also lost some of its power. True, young people do speak a good deal about self-fulfillment. But self-fulfillment for them does not consist in the acquisition of certain determinate perfections or in the realization of some determinate ideal. Self-fulfillment signifies for them, first of all, their refusal to view life as a matter of integrating themselves in some pre-existing structure. They want, as they say, to be themselves. Just what this means positively, however, they are hard put to define. One thing is certain—they do not want to be alone. Their new sense of responsibility has heightened their feeling of loneliness and isolation. Hence their constant talk about their need for other people, of broadening their experience, and of achieving some kind of community. Life as the pursuit of perfection seems to them much too private an affair to be able to cure them of that isolation from which they so desperately desire to be delivered.

Responsibility Itself as the Controlling Image

In the present context the symbol of responsibility has itself assumed a certain ascendancy as a way of interpreting man's life. The late Dr. H. Richard Niebuhr has done perhaps more than anyone else to develop this symbol thematically.

According to Dr. Niebuhr, man's life is essentially a matter of interaction. It is less a business of pursuing goods or of conforming to laws than it is of responding to actions upon us. Moreover, man's response to the actions of others proceeds in the light of his understanding of them. This understanding or interpretation of what is going on may be more or less adequate. It is, indeed, the business of thought to make the interpretation as adequate as possible. Thought by itself, however, is never sufficient. In addition to his habitual understanding of the situation, a man must bring to each encounter what Professor Tillich has called a *listening* love. If his response is to be adequate, it must be in terms of what is here and now being said to him.

Besides, however, being reactions to interpreted actions upon us, our own actions, as responsible, must also be made in anticipation of answers to our answers. As Dr. Niebuhr remarks: "An agent's action is like a statement in a dialogue. Such a statement not only seeks to meet, as it were, or to fit into, the previous statement to which it is an answer, but is made in anticipation of reply. It looks forward as well as backward; it anticipates objections, confirmations, and corrections. It is made as part of a total conversation that leads forward and is to have meaning as a whole. . . . So considered, no action taken as an atomic unit is responsible. Responsibility lies in the agent who stays with his action, who accepts the consequences in the form of reactions, and looks forward in a present deed to the continued interaction." [1]

This brings up the final component of the notion of responsibility; namely, the component of social solidarity. "Our action is responsible when it is a response to action upon us in a continuing discourse or interaction among beings forming a continuing society. . . . Personal responsibility [thus] implies the continuity of a self . . . in the community of agents to which response is being made. There could be no responsible self in an interaction in which the reaction to one's response comes from a source wholly different from that whence the original action issued." [2]

Bringing all this together, we have Niebuhr's definition of re-

[1] H. Richard Niebuhr, *The Responsible Self* (New York: Harper & Row, 1963), p. 64.
[2] *Ibid.*, p. 65.

sponsibility. It is, he says, "the idea of an agent's action as response to an action upon him in accordance with his interpretation of the latter action and with his expectation of response to his response; and all of this is in a continuing community of agents." [3]

In the light of this image of *man-the-responder*, we can see more precisely the inadequacies of those former images; namely, the image of *man-the-maker*, bent on making something out of life and seeing his environment only in terms of its usefulness; and of *man-the-citizen*, whose life is one of obedience to laws and who feels threatened when the laws are questioned. To be a responder in a conversation is to participate in something that is not all worked out beforehand. Indeed, if the participants in a conversation come to it with preconceived ideas about what the conclusion should be, the conversation will never really begin. Again, if we may speak of such things as rules of conversing, their function is not to determine the outcome of the dialogue but only to make it possible. The important thing in a conversation is for each participant really to listen to what the other is saying, to be aware of being spoken to, and to make the fitting response. Nor will this be something he thought up beforehand; it will be that precisely which takes up the other's lead and moves the talk forward.

Metaphysical Implications

The image of responsibility involves a certain metaphysical understanding of reality as it is disclosed in human experience. It is precisely a metaphysics of selfhood. It sees the real as made up of individual and original centers or powers of action, involved existentially in a field of interaction but not systematically related to one another. No matter how determinate the individual natures may be, these natures do not determine what they shall encounter nor what the outcome of their many encounters shall be. Each is

[3] *Ibid.*

thus viewed as radically contingent, that is to say, as a being that can exist only by contact with what is not itself, a contact indeed which is often a collision.

They are, moreover, caught up in a timeful drama whose outcome is unforeseeable. The totality of self and other, whose interaction makes up the real, cannot be thought of as forming a timeless whole. The wholeness of reality is not the wholeness of an organism nor a system whose elements are all parts of one and the same. Such a conception would destroy not only the otherness of the other but the very selfhood of the self. The wholeness of reality is rather that precisely of an ongoing encounter in which the other continually comes to the self to become part of its history. The other is precisely that *which comes*, that is, the future (*à venir*), and the individual's response to what comes engenders his past.

Finally, as constituted by the interaction of original powers, reality must be thought of as fraught with novelty and as genuinely creative. What occurs cannot be viewed as a simple unfolding of a given nature; it is, rather, the issue of a true encounter. It depends on what meetings take place and how they proceed. The concrete synthesis, therefore, achieved through interaction does not pre-exist its own accomplishment and is strictly unpredictable.

If we may speak of a law presiding over this development, it is not the law of any determinate nature but is that of *Being* itself which is beyond all determinations. This is the law of Being's self-affirmation as an absolute, all-inclusive value in which everything that is participates and according to which each individual, in its action, seeks not merely his own promotion but the promotion of the other as well. The action of any individual is not merely a matter of self-affirmation in isolation; it is the affirmation of itself in relation to the other. That is to say, it is the affirmation of itself in a state of synthesis in which both itself and the other, which it needs for its own existence, are preserved in their integrity.

In human terms this comes down to the affirmation of community. The exigencies, therefore, that we ought to meet in our personal conduct are not the exigencies merely of any particular nature; they are, rather, the exigencies of interpersonal community. That action is right which maintains and promotes the community of persons; that action is wrong which disrupts or jeopardizes it. Similarly, the good that we seek as persons is not a good that can be privately achieved. Nor is it to be identified with any settled or determinate state of affairs. The good that we seek is precisely the good of community, that reality which includes each of us in his originality and at the same time heals him of his isolation.

This reality of community is never a mere matter of fact. It is fundamentally a task that must be begun with the dawn of each day. If we may, and indeed must, deliberately intend it, we can do so only by being open and responsive to the other as it comes to us and by seeking to meet it on its own terms. The law of our actions thus becomes the law of love, and its goal is a living and vital relationship with the other as other.

Thus, while the image of *man-the-responder* transcends the older images of *man-the-maker*, the purposeful pursuer of determinate goals, and of *man-the-citizen*, obedient to determinate laws, it does not wholly abandon them but rather lifts them to a new level of significance. What it does is to take them out of the realm of the determinate and matter of fact and lift them into the realm of the indeterminate by excess, the realm of Being itself, which is the true abode of man as person.

Responsibility and Authority

We are now in a position to take up the question with which we started. The existence of authority in a community has always been justified by the need which the community has of it if the community is to be able to exist at all. Only if there is a central power, capable of coordinating the activities of all the individuals who go to make up the community in view of the achievement of their common life, which is the inclusive good of all concerned, can such a common good come into being.

Obedience to legitimate authority has likewise been justified on the same basis. If the individual's subordination of himself in his actions to the dictates of legitimate authority involves a certain alienation from himself (in a sense that the initiative for the particular course he follows lies in a source outside himself), this alienation is only temporary and provisional. He is justified in following the lead of another insofar precisely as such submission is required for the achievement of the common good—a good which precisely as common is also his own.

With this position, as far as it goes, we have no quarrel. It should be noted, however, that it merely vindicates the existence of authority in general and the individual's general subordination to the exercise of legitimate authority. It does not concern itself with what the individual's response should be in the face of any particular directive. Yet precisely here is where the difficulties arise. Nor are these difficulties resolved by any attempt to convert this general theory into a norm for concrete practice. This, I think, is where much traditional thinking about the relationship between authority and the individuals under it often goes astray. The abstract conception of authority as the right to command, to which there corresponds an obligation in the subordinate to obey, is made into a proximate rule of moral behavior. Thus the only proper response in the face of a directive issued by legitimate authority is one of submission. Whatever ideas or feelings the individual may have which are contrary to the directive are thought to be irrelevant.

The action of authority is thus pictured as a one-way affair. It proceeds from an "unmoved mover" to a being who, if he behaves properly, allows himself to be shaped by that movement and offers no resistance. In relation to authority the individual is the "wholly moved."

The mistake of this view is twofold. First of all, it makes the individual's relation to the common good wholly passive. It forgets that he is an active power of being and that, as involved in interaction, he is necessarily concerned not merely with the promotion of his own particular good but with the furtherance of community as well. Since he remains responsible for his actions and their effect on community, he can never abstain from judging whether or not a particular directive is really in the service of community nor from acting in accord with this judgment.

Second, the view is mistaken because it abstracts authority from the concrete context in which it actually exists. It forgets that authority, existing as a center of power in a concrete field of interaction, is not systematically or determinately related to the achievement of the common good. It is itself subject to all sorts of pressures and influences, including the weight of sheer inertia, which may have as much to do with the actual shaping of its directives as its desire for the promotion of community.

This being the case, a purely passive stance in the presence of authority would be the height of irresponsibility. If the proper stance of the individual in relation to authority may be described as one of obedience, then this obedience can never be unquestioning. Instead of being a matter of mere submission, it is much more a habit of cooperative interaction. The obedient man is the one who cooperates with authority in the sense that he makes its aims his own and respects authority as a necessary means for the attainment of those aims. Even when his interaction takes the form of opposition to a particular directive, this opposition never looks to the abrogation of authority but rather to its strengthening, to helping it overcome its own failures and limitations in its actual exercise.

The proper course to be followed, therefore, in the presence of any particular directive, must be decided by the individual in the same way as he decides his course in the case of any other interaction. His response to the action of authority should be such that, all things considered, it promotes rather than hinders the advance of genuine community. If he does this, he will not only be able to give an answer for all his actions, but will also be showing all the respect that is due to authority.

So to conceive the individual's relation to authority, that is, as one of cooperative interaction for the promotion of the common good, is not to lighten his load. On the contrary, it puts upon him the burden not only of taking a continually active stance, but of acting also always in the light of love. The achievement of such love will, it is obvious, demand of him a constant process of purification from any form of egoism. If he is called to take a constructively critical attitude toward authority, his stance toward himself must be one of even more unremitting criticism.

On the other hand, this conception likewise makes the role of authority somewhat more difficult than those in authority frequently like to portray it. In the face of *active* individuals, who are conscious of their own power and responsibility, authority cannot content itself with the role of merely issuing directives. It must have ears as well as a tongue. Since its actions, too, should proceed from love and not from the mere urge to dominate, it must open itself to criticism. Only if it, too, learns to listen will it be able to give the response which the situation calls for.

We are said today to be living in an age of renewal, both inside and outside the Church. It is an age of renewal and not only of change, insofar as it involves the effort to give new shape and expression to the transcendent structures and values which traditional forms were meant to express and promote, but now too often seem to betray. That this effort has been stimulated and fostered "from the bottom up," that is to say, by those under authority rather than by authority itself, is no secret. In other words, in actual practice, the relationship between the governed and the governors seems pretty much as we have described it here. It is not the one-way street so often pictured by moralists. It has, rather, the structure of a genuine encounter; a truly creative moment from which something new and good can emerge that neither side by itself could wholly anticipate or plan. Perhaps, therefore, while we are renewing everything else, we may also renew our ideas on this matter and bring them into accord with reality.

FREEDOM AND THE LAYMAN

DANIEL CALLAHAN

If it is true, as Karl Rahner has written, that "the layman is a Christian who remains in the world," it might then follow that a layman would be wise to discuss freedom from his vantage point in the world. That is what I propose to do. But more than common prudence commends this course. For it is daily borne in upon a layman that he is caught between two realms. On the one hand there is the accumulated wisdom of the Church, conveyed to him in his religious education, through the liturgy, in sermons and exhortations. To this may be added the growing body of literature on the "theology of the layman." On the other hand there is the accumulated wisdom of the secular world; here is another master which daily instructs him. Ideally, the Church should give the layman some insight into the meaning of that world in which he lives. Practically speaking, however, it often happens that the world, in turn, gives the layman some insight into the meaning of the Church. There is really nothing odd in this, much less anything improper. The wise man will take his wisdom wherever he finds it, and so should the Church.

The subject at hand is "freedom and the layman." It is at once possible to see that the contemporary pertinence of this subject tells us as much about the world as it does about the Church. History is not just a series of accidents, whether it is a matter of secular or ecclesiastical history. And here history shows us that the emerging consciousness of twentieth-century man has come to center on the idea of freedom. The sources of this emergence are many. There is, in impulse at least, a movement away from paternalistic societies, stimulated in great part by the spread of democratic ideals throughout the world. Even the most autocratic political regimes feel compelled to pay homage to the goal of the self-directing free man in a free society. This movement toward human autonomy has been powerfully prodded by the disastrous consequences of man's recent experience with totalitarian governments. There is, quite rightly, a deep and pervasive suspicion of any theory of government which assumes that men should place their fate totally in the hands of others. This does not mean that men do not in fact still do so; but as a general theory any paternalistic ideology has come upon hard days.

Closely related to this development is an awakening consciousness of the responsibility of the person to make his own moral decisions. In the Nuremberg trials and in the case of Adolf Eichmann, the world saw the utterly evil consequences of an ethic which enables men to excuse their crimes against humanity on the grounds that they are merely "following orders." Here were men—men as self-excusing animals—who declared that they had no obligation to determine matters of right and wrong. Their only duty, as they saw it, was to be loyal and obedient servants of the regime to which they had pledged allegiance. The moral, for those who would call themselves free men, was clear: there is no cause, no loyalty, no set of principles which can justify any person who would claim he is not responsible for his actions. Not one of us can hand over his moral decisions to another.

Still another source of the emergence of freedom as the rallying cry of our day is the suffocating presence of mass societies. We no longer live in a world of scattered individuals clustered together in small groups, surrounded by unmapped wilderness and virgin forests. Now there are people everywhere, so many, indeed, that it is more and more difficult for the individual to keep himself from being swallowed up in an endless sea of nameless humanity. Impersonal economic, political, and sociological forces frighten and coerce us. Faced with such forces, we seek personal initiative, personal identification, and personal freedom with desperate energy. So, too, in such a world, there is much talk of self-fulfillment, honesty, integrity, authenticity—talk, that is, of anything which will help the isolated individual retain some vital sense of his uniqueness, his right to existence, his personal worth and destiny.

There is a connecting thread which binds together the seemingly disparate movements and events which are shaking the contemporary world. The African who rebels against colonialism is moved by many of the same deep forces which impel the Negro in Harlem to force out white merchants. The novelist who glorifies a life of sexual abandon and despises the mores of middle-class monogamy shares a certain kinship with the Christian social reformer who would uproot a system of exploitation based on ritualistically accepted economic values. Each protests against a passive acquiescence to unexamined cultural values. The local communist party leader who desires some degree of independence from Moscow is stirred by a spirit not wholly unlike that which leads many students today to rebel against authority. The connecting thread in all of these instances is a surge toward freedom, however misguided and naïve may be the forms it takes.

Freedom is in the bones of modern man; one way or another it will find expression. He wants freedom from hunger, from political domination, from the impersonal weight of oppressive custom and ritualistically sustained values. He wants freedom to plan his own life, to make his own decisions, to find that mode and direction of life which will enable him to realize his full human dignity. But modern man is also skeptical, less given to utopian dreams, less prone to place his faith in charismatic leaders, less willing to commit himself blindly to the panaceas of those who would call themselves wise. He is often a rebel, burned and scarred by the ravages of too many holy wars, too many causes turned sour, too many dreams shattered. To be sure, in moments of fear or in moments of sudden vision the rebel in him may give way to the conformist or the enthusiast; but the rebel is still there, ready to reappear when calm returns or the vision fades. Above all, he wants to be himself, and that self, he has found, can be achieved only through freedom.

What, in the judgment of modern man, are the conditions necessary to insure this freedom he seeks? One can discern something approaching a consensus in answer to this question. At its focal point is the possibility of making choices. The measure of freedom is the psychological capacity to choose between alternative possibilities and the presence of genuine options from which to choose. There is a desire for political freedom—the freedom to choose among a variety of political goals and programs. There is a desire for social freedom—the freedom to choose among different styles of life. There is a desire for psychological freedom—the freedom to chart one's own course free of open or hidden conditioning pressures. There is a desire for religious freedom—the freedom to search out God in one's own way, and, if no God can be found, the freedom to live a life which has no transcendent good at its center. So put, there are fewer and fewer men in our world who would dissent from this consensus.

Something more must be said here. It is not enough for modern man that this freedom be theoretically available; not enough that his nation boast a beautifully conceived constitution guaranteeing his rights; not enough that his church have a theology which vindicates his freedom of conscience; not enough that the savants deplore undue social, economic, and cultural coercion. What matters is that man's freedom be real, concrete, and effective, a freedom which can be exercised openly, safely, and fully. The Negro in America has constitutional freedoms, but he often does not have real freedom. The religious believer in the Soviet Union has legally guaranteed rights, but he cannot freely exercise these rights without paying a penalty. The poverty-stricken slum dweller in Latin America has the social right to economic mobility and a decent life, but those who control the wealth do not give him the opportunity to realize this right. If modern man is a skeptic, he is especially distrustful of paper values, good only for looking and not for acting.

The contemporary world has been a hard school. About man's freedom it has taught him to beware of absolutes, whether these absolutes be ideological, spiritual, moral, or political. Above all, it has taught him to be excessively wary of giving his wholehearted allegiance to any scheme of values which entails that he sacrifice his independence and his freedom of choice and judgment. Politically, he has learned that his freedom is safe only where power is relative, subject to checks and balances, limited in scope and application. Ideologically, he has learned that there exists no cause which is more valuable than the good of the individual; men do not exist to be sacrificed for abstractions, even if labeled "humanity." Morally, he has learned that ethical values often reflect nothing more than regional traditions, tribal customs, the mores of ruling elites, and the vestigial habits of dead generations. Theologically, he has learned that men often make God in their own image, domesticating religion so that it may better serve, justify, and rationalize the *status quo* of society.

So much, then, for the lessons of the contemporary world. To the extent that the Catholic lives in this world and breathes its air, he will have been tutored along with all other men. Perhaps it is true that this education has been mainly negative, telling man more what to avoid than what to seek. Perhaps it is true that, in an age when old certainties are losing their savor, man is left without a mooring, turned back in upon himself and doomed to seek an elusive selfhood. Perhaps so, but he cannot for all that ignore what he has learned.

Now let us turn to that world which the Church represents, that other spiritual space in which the layman exists. For one who has taken seriously the lessons of the secular world, the contrast is striking. Here is an institution which, it is commonly believed, demands of its members absolute submission, absolute commit ment; hence it rejects that wisdom which warns that loyalties should always be provisional. Here is an organization which has at its head a human being of whom the astounding claim is made that, on occasion, he is absolutely protected from error; hence it ignores the advice to be wary of those leaders whose followers argue that he is one set apart from ordinary, finite humanity. Here is a community of men which, in its manuals, proclaims the freedom of man's conscience, but which in the past has been known to advocate the burning of dissidents and even now is perfectly willing to banish the heretic into the outer darkness; hence it exhibits one important characteristic of those totalitarian states with an official party line. Here is a social structure which, far from having a system of checks and balances, centers power in the hands of a few men only, men not chosen for their office by those whom they command, and men from whose decisions there is no higher recourse; hence it ignores the experience of a humanity which has suffered at the hands of sovereign lords and dictators.

This list need not be continued. Its thrust should be clear. What are we to say at this point? We could say that what is true in the world is not true in the Church, that what is valuable wisdom for man in his political life does not apply in the Church. But this will not do. The Church has always been able to profit from the conclusions of reasonable men meditating on human existence; it should be able to profit in this instance. Nor can we be so naïve as to think that the ills which afflict the secular world cannot afflict the Church. The Church is made up of men, and it will show the marks of their humanity. Or we could say that the world is correct in its hard-won truths about freedom, but that the Church is so unique an institution that these truths can safely be ignored. Here we might say: Yes, let man be wary of those who claim to have a special access to truth; but let him make an exception in the case of the Church's claims. Yes, let men reject systems of government which contain no checks and balances on the exercise of power; but let him accept the absolute power of the Church, for in that exceptional instance the authority to command obedience comes directly from God. Yes, let no man form his conscience according to the commands of others or suspend his right to absolute moral choice—except in that unique case where the Church teaches one what to choose. These stratagems will not do either.

The difference between the Church and a totalitarian government cannot simply turn on the fact that the former preaches the truth and the latter falsehood. It cannot turn on an assertion that a person should hold on to his freedom when a dictator would take it from him, but should give it up if the Church bids him to do so. It cannot turn on a claim to freedom of choice in the face of a monolithic society, but allow a relinquishment of that freedom when the monolith happens to be a church.

The difference between the Church and an absolutist system of political power must be so sharp there can be no question of making "distinctions" of the kind cited above. In recent decades much has been done and said to allay the fear of non-Catholics that the Church is essentially a many-tentacled, power-hungry monster. Yet it has by no means convinced the world that the values it represents in the province of authority—absolute commitment to absolute truth mediated by men with absolute power—is compatible with freedom and human dignity. Those who exercise authority may be benevolent, enlightened, sensitive, humble, self-effacing. For all that, and even granting the many limitations on ecclesiastical authority which Catholic theology recognizes, there remains a residue of absolutism. And absolutism, whatever the form it may take, represents a potential danger to freedom, a danger verified by history time and again. At the moment the world looks upon the Church as an ally; now the Church stands with the freedom of man. But it has not always done so in the past. As for the future—who can tell? That is why the Church remains an object of suspicion.

Let me add a prediction here. No matter how strongly the Council may affirm religious liberty and freedom of conscience, the wariness and suspicion will remain. For from the viewpoint of the world the Church still claims a special access to truth and a special mandate to proclaim that truth in a binding way. For all the world can see there is nothing in logic or history which would make it impossible for a future Council to overturn the work of the present Council; or for future popes to declare that the work of our contemporary popes was a mistake. If Catholic thought can change once on religious liberty it can change again. The Catholic may protest here, simply asserting that the Church will not regress. But he cannot prove it, and he surely is not prophetic enough to speak with absolute confidence about the thought of a Council or pope one, two, or three centuries from now. The world thinks it sees absolutism, and it has learned to its great cost that with absolutism all things are possible.

Enough has been said here to indicate a problem of considerable magnitude. A number of questions arise. Is it time, as the world is now coming to hold, that any institution or system of thought which contains an element of absolutism constitutes a potential danger to freedom? If this is so, does that word "any" actually include *even* the Church? Is it further true that any man who commits himself totally to a system of values, an institution, or a church, is no longer a free man? (It will not do here quickly to answer that as long as his absolute commitment was a matter of free choice no problem of freedom need arise. Many men joined the SS of their own free choice.) Is it true that the sensible man, one who has learned the lessons of history well, is a person skeptical of all absolute values, absolute authorities, absolute truths? If this is true, does that mean that the Catholic is, by definition, one who is not wise? I will not try to answer these questions directly, for I doubt that such is what the situation demands. Any Catholic with a minimal training in philosophy and theology could unearth some old sayings or propositions to handle them, but that method has been tried and found wanting.

Let me, instead, suggest that the Church must try to give the world not only nicely reasoned theological positions, but also a new experience, by word and deed, of the compatibility of freedom and commitment, of freedom and strong authority, of freedom and the acceptance of values which do not spring wholly from human creativity. The Christian must always affirm that an acceptance of Christ is a total acceptance. It cannot be provisional or tentative; if it is, it is not faith of the kind Christ asked of men. Moreover, the Catholic must hold that the acceptance of the authority of the Church is inextricably bound up with his faith in Christ; and this means accepting fully the authority of those who speak in Christ's name. Finally, commitment to Christ and His Church means that one accepts the revelation of Christ's life, death, and resurrection and the values, stemming wholly from God, which the event of that revelation carries with it. In the face of the wisdom of the world, however, it is no good just to assert these things, much less to assert that no danger to freedom arises. The world must, somehow, see for itself. It must see with its own eyes the fact of Catholics acting freely, experiencing freedom, standing forth as witnesses to freedom.

The reason why the Church must enable men to see freedom does not entirely turn upon the necessary apostolic goal of drawing all men to Christ. It also turns upon the need of the world for positive examples, creative insights, and workable suggestions which would assist it in resolving some of its own, purely temporal dilemmas, especially those concerning the relationship of one human being with another. I have mentioned that mankind has become skeptical of absolutist political systems, moral and spiritual values. While this is, I think, a valid observation, one can also observe that few men are happy living in a universe which requires unremitting cynicism and skepticism. Human beings do want values; they do want goals toward which they can strive. They have learned to be suspicious of those men and groups proclaiming that they alone possess the truth, but they still show every sign of wanting to find the truth. In civic life enlightened men do not want dictatorships or military rule; but they do want firm, positive reasons for obeying legitimate laws. In education students less and less want autocratic teachers presenting them with ready-made truth; but they do want to believe there remains the possibility of discovering truth. In ethics men no longer want detailed lists of moral injunctions; but they do want some sense that moral values have an intrinsic meaning and man's dignity some transcendent significance.

All of this is only to say that the world is confused. It has learned some of its lessons well, and conclusions have been drawn. Yet it has not learned where to go from here. That is why the freedom of the layman has a special importance: as a test case of whether there exists the possibility of a total commitment which remains fully compatible with human freedom. If there does exist such a possibility, to be found in a commitment to Christ and His Church, then it ought to be possible to realize man's freedom in the Christian life. The alternative is ominous. If freedom cannot be realized in the Christian life, a life grounded on the profound conviction that man is free and is made in the image of God, then it is hard to see how it can be realized anywhere else. Much, then, is at stake in the way the Church comes to work out the freedom of the layman: a viable example for the world, the Church's effectiveness in witnessing to the freedom of the children of God, and the possibility of the efficacious presence of the Church among men.

Before suggesting how the Church might demonstrate, in the life of the layman, the possibility of freedom joined with commitment, let me confess to a considerable uneasiness. I do not have a clear vision of a perfect resolution of the apparently conflicting demands posed by the world's perception of the conditions required for freedom and by the Church's call to faith and obedience. Like many another lay Catholic, I suspect, I see the persuasiveness of each claim; but the key to their ultimate reconciliation escapes me. Yet to say as much will, I hope, help to set the tone of the inquiry. If the layman is to make any contribution in working out these complicated puzzles, a good place to start is by admitting the gaps in his perception.

Nonetheless, there are many pointers toward a reconciliation available in the Church of Vatican II. Taken together they may be able to provide the ingredients of a solution.

1. The most important advance of the contemporary Church lies in the dawning recognition that Christianity has as its sole end and meaning the encounter of the human person with the person of Christ; and through Christ, in the Spirit, with God the Father. This point need not be elaborated here. It will suffice only to note that this recognition shifts the emphasis of the Christian life away from a law-centered spirituality to a spirituality of personal growth in holiness. Law is not denied; instead, it is put into a new perspective. Most importantly, the layman is put in a better position to understand the uniqueness of his relationship with God—to understand, that is, how radically different love of God and His Church is from loyalty to a temporal ruler and a secular institution.

2. This uniqueness is emphasized by a fresh awareness of the work of the Holy Spirit in the life of the individual. I think it fair to say that, at least in the recent past, the layman believed the Holy Spirit could move him only through the mediation of the teaching authority of the Church. In short, what did not proceed from authority, or did not have the sanction of authority, was thought worthy of suspicion. Hence the perfect layman did not initiate, he only followed. Today, by contrast, we are coming to see that the Holy Spirit can work through the individual layman, not only on occasion by leading him to enlighten or rebuke authority, but also by impelling him to act freely in the service of Christ. The Spirit is present in the whole Church, that is, in each person in the Church.

3. The whole Church is the People of God. That means the Church is a community, made up of people each with different gifts, vocations, and functions, but each sharing a common human-

ity, equality, and destiny in the eyes of God. Some will have the power of orders (priests); some will have the powers of jurisdiction (bishops and popes); some will have neither of these powers (the laity). Nonetheless, these different functions do not disturb the Christian equality of each person; and that is a significant basis for personal freedom. Even amid a hierarchical order, Christian equality implies a fraternal relationship of those teaching and those taught, of ruler and ruled. Those who rule can only do so by serving, and the spirit of service will be demonstrated by humility and openness.

4. Humility and openness, however, should spring from motives fuller than a spirit of childlike simplicity which should be the mark of all Christians. For one who holds authority there should be a deep appreciation of the inescapable fact that only God is our Lord. The authority of a pope, of a bishop, is only a relative authority, given by God, subject to God. In theory there is no difficulty here, but practice is another matter. The Church has always been subject to the temptations of the world, and nowhere has this been more evident than in the tendency of ecclesiastical authority to effect the manner and airs of the absolute secular ruler (and, by and large, the people have approved). Perhaps now the Church is coming to see that, however understandable this tendency, it ill befits an authority whose very presence must symbolize a total submission to God. But this is all of a piece with perceiving that authority in the Church can neither be likened to, nor should it emulate, any other system of authority in the world.

5. It is that latter perception which, little by little, is coming to reshape Catholic education. The shrewd secular ruler has long known that conditioned responses are supremely useful tools for shaping a docile and uncritically loyal populace. The Church, to put it gently, has not always disdained a use of these tools. An emphasis on conformity to Church law, a rigorous system of school and Church discipline, a dependence on external sanctions, a triumphalistic reciting of institutional glories, a suspicion of the

original mind, a suppression of dissenters, a doting upon letter-perfect orthodoxy, a will-centered morality, a glorification of the submissive personality—all of these things have been characteristic of Catholic life and thought for centuries. Today they are slowly being rejected, although the changing of catechetical and juridical methods is by no means an easy matter.

6. Of no slight importance here is the revolution which has taken place in the Church's understanding of religious liberty. By and large, the great conciliar and pre-conciliar debates on religious liberty turned on the problem of the religious liberty of non-Catholics. This was only natural. The rise of the pluralistic state and the favored place of democratic forms of government combined with a widespread legal separation of Church and state brought the nineteenth-century position of the Church under heavy fire. No longer does the Church talk the language of "thesis-hypothesis." No longer does one hear that "error has no rights" (a meaningless expression, anyway). Instead, the liberty of all men to seek God and to worship Him in their own way is proclaimed—or not to seek Him and not to worship Him.

But one can hardly discuss the liberty of non-Catholics without, by implication, saying something about the religious liberty of Catholics. For if the non-Catholic must be allowed to follow his conscience, then so surely must the Catholic. That means the conscience of the Catholic dissenter, even of the apostate and the heretic, must be respected. Although this implication of a full understanding of religious liberty is still rarely discussed, it looms on the horizon. The fact that the Church has been slow of late in condemning doctrinal aberrations, willing to tolerate bold new lines of theological speculation, and reluctant to resort to excommunication, suggests that practice is now well ahead of theory. The result one might hope for is the minimizing of impossible choices; that is, situations in which the Catholic believes himself forced to choose between suppressing honest doubts about this or that article of the faith (and thus being dishonest with himself and others) and leaving the Church.

7. These relatively abstract pointers toward freedom need to be complemented by some specific institutions designed to promote and insure freedom. There is considerable merit in the numerous suggestions for giving laymen a legally established and guaranteed right to be heard in the Church. It is of no use assuring the layman that his voice counts if there is no way in which it can be heard and no obligation on the part of authority to listen. The development of a body of lay theologians, the presence of laymen in diocesan synods, in Roman offices, on conciliar commissions, in administrative positions in Catholic education—the list of possibilities is endless—will insure a hearing for lay opinion. To this list should be added a canonically guaranteed right to petition (easily) for the redress of grievances, the right to full information on Church finances and procedures, the right of public protest against abuses of authority—again, the possibilities are infinite.

One might aptly observe at this point that the laity already have a considerable voice and influence. Despite some grumbling, the recent outbursts of lay criticism and suggestion have been tolerated, even encouraged; there have been no significant reprisals, no monitums, no silencings. Moreover, the conciliar debates have given every indication that the Fathers have listened, and responded, to the laity. But it is important to bear in mind that all of this progress has been achieved more or less by accident; or, better, one would like to say, through the unexpected workings of the Holy Spirit. There is nothing yet in the *structure* of the Church which provides for the guaranteed continuation of this permissiveness, this creative listening on the part of the hierarchy which we are now experiencing. Little imagination is required to envision the possibilty of another generation of popes and bishops deciding that the laity ought, once again, to be seen and not heard. There is nothing in the juridical workings of the Church to prevent such a reversal, nor much at this point that the laity could do to stop it. That possibility entails the necessity of written rights and guarantees. The freedom of the laity should never again be dependent upon the mood of a historical moment, or upon the charitable toleration of those who rule. As the Chinese know, those who have the unilateral power magnanimously to allow one hundred flowers to bloom also have the power to uproot them.

These seven pointers (and one might list others) seem to me to provide the main elements of a solution to the dilemma of freedom and authority. If this can be done, then one word I used earlier should no longer have any meaningful sense with reference to the Church: the word "absolute." At the present time it still remains possible to talk of *absolute* power in the Church and of the Catholic as an absolutist. But the word ought to have an alien ring to the Christian; and if the Christian manages to be what he should be, then they should seem to all men inappropriate words to use when speaking of one who follows Christ.

How could men ever describe as absolutists those who commit themselves to Christ as free men, giving themselves to Him who loves them? Or those who freely belong to a community radically rooted in human dignity and equality? Or those who believe that the Spirit can blow where it will, directly illuminating even the least gifted among us? Or those who reject with a passion the manipulating of the mind and the conditioning of the emotions? Or those for whom the dissenter is not the enemy but rather the suffering brother or the prophetic brother? Or those who look upon religious liberty as a sacred right, to be taken from no man? Or those who, in their institutions and legal structures, have provided clear safeguards against the abuse of authority? Or those who, whatever their position, never forget that all they have comes from God?

Let me put aside theological definitions of the layman. Let me, instead, call him Everyman. He is the man who, in political society, is only a statistic, his person all but invisible to the naked eye, the victim of forces he cannot control, leaders he cannot influence, and a history he did not make. The critical problem of our age of the mass society is to recognize his existence, to give flesh and blood and freedom to him as a person. One would like to say the problem is totally different within the Church, but it is not. That is why the achieving of freedom for the layman in the Church could have a meaning which goes well beyond the Church. For if it is not possible for a Christian to be free in a community of Christians, then it is unlikely that any man will for long be free in any kind of community. What is it for a man to be free? Now we have to answer that question with words. Someday, perhaps, we will be able to answer it merely by picking out a layman at random and pointing to him. Words are not needed when the eye can see.

Possibilities of Freedom
in Tomorrow's Complex Society

Jean-Yves Calvez, S.J.

The reason which has led to the selection of my topic is probably not confidence but rather anxiety. There is indeed a challenge to freedom in our present and coming society; there is even an already full-blown and deeply seated crisis of freedom. I must briefly refer to it, before attempting an appraisal of the opportunities offered by tomorrow's complex societies and the determination of the means by which we can cope with the challenge implicit in the probable features of such societies.

To begin with, I wish to allude to Pope John XXIII's treatment of the subject in his encyclical *Mater et Magistra*. Never before had a pope shown himself so conscious of the growing complexity of our social life. Pope John's concern has been translated into many languages by the word "socialization." As a matter of fact, in English-speaking countries that expression has sometimes been carefully excluded, in order to avoid misrepresentation, especially an identification between the facts alluded at by the Pope and the socialist principle of systematic nationalization or collectivization of the means of production. The expression "socialization" also has a specific meaning in psychology. Still, I believe that there is a reverse danger in not using that expression or a similar one: those who try to avoid it in their translations sometimes are running the risk of misunderstanding the amplitude of the social transformation considered by John XXIII. Some of them seem to reduce this transformation to the vulgar fact of a multiplication of associations and social institutions in which men nowadays become involved. Pope John XXIII thought of this, of course, but he was aware of a wider and deeper process: "The *interdependence* of citizens," he said, "becomes daily more complex." [1] And he added: "This growth in the intricacy of social relationships is both a sign and a cause of the increasingly widening scope of state intervention in matters which, since they touch the intimate affairs of the human person, are certainly not of little account nor without danger. The state may, for example, concern itself with care for the sick, training and education of the young, choice of a career, and the rehabilitation or remedial treatment of mental or physical disability" (*Mater et Magistra*, Number 60).

Socialization also consists—and perhaps even today mainly consists—in the progress of communication between men. John XXIII also took notice of this: "The new and ever improving means of communicating ideas, by print, cinema, radio, and television give people the power to be present, as it were, at events in any part of the world, no matter how distant" (*Mater et Magistra*, Number 61). A little more than a century ago Marx and Saint-Simon described the first phase of modern socialization: a revolutionary social division of labor which socialized the process of production. At that time few people, not even the socialists, thought of a socialization covering all other aspects of man's life: consumption, dwelling, culture, and leisure. Socialization has become all-pervasive today; thus the impression of a thoroughly socialized life, of a life entirely penetrated by society no longer stops at the threshold of the factory.

Taking all this into view, John XXIII, although an optimist in many ways, wrote: "The daily growth in number, scale, and variety of such societies (which surround us more and more) has the consequence that in many of these fields of activity there is a

---

[1] *Mater et Magistra*, translation by J. R. Kirwan, "The Social Thought of John XXIII." Catholic Social Guild, Oxford, 1964, Number 59.

multiplication of rules and laws to govern and define the mutual relationships of citizens. Each and every man has his scope for freedom of action narrowed: means are used, ways are followed, such a state of affairs is brought into existence, as to render it difficult for anyone to make decisions of his own unaffected by influences from outside, to use his initiative, to maintain his rights and duties as he ought, to exercise and perfect his innate powers" (*Mater et Magistra,* Number 62). Pope John XXIII was thus voicing the fears of an age, or rather of the conscious ones in an age which would tend to make the majority of men unconscious of self and incapable of responsible conduct.

There is indeed a crisis of freedom. Twenty years after a cruel war and the revelation of Nazi and Soviet concentration camps, ten or twelve years after the end of the Zhdanov era and of Stalin's dictatorship, we still cannot forget that oppression of freedom of world dimensions, perhaps the ugliest of all time, which happened in our own lifetime. Even today violations of basic liberties are common; they may be of lesser scope, but they are also treated with less indignation. They are not unknown—we read about them in our daily papers—but they are, so to speak, unnoticed. One remembers, in ironic contrast, the furious indignation, be it somewhat romantic, which flared up a century ago when the news spread of the massacre of the Armenians.

Worse, there is in many circles a growing indifference toward freedom. Liberal parties in many parts of the world have vanished or lost their prestige; not only in Great Britain or continental Europe, but also in South America. Recently the "free world" motto, used in the cold war between West and East was accepted only with reluctance and suspicion in many circles of Western countries: it sounded to some as insufficient to inspire courage or to suggest the values to be defended in that conflict. It has not played the role which the appeal to liberty played in the eighteenth or nineteenth centuries. In many new free and independent countries the leaders pay scant attention to the freedom of citizens; they do not consider freedom a political asset. Their major problem, at times, is rather what amount of tolerable coercion they can impose upon their peoples in order to meet the requirements of economic development; and they are sometimes encouraged to impose a maximum restriction of freedom by their foreign economic and political advisers, not only those from the communist countries but also from Western states. A few years ago Guinea's President Sekou Toure even took pride in being the first African leader to have reintroduced forced labor in an independent African state.

We may also take examples from other parts of the world. Among various categories of people, either union leaders or—even more—intellectuals, there is a constant expression of the necessity of an imperative (strictly binding) planned society instead of an indicative one, or instead of the planning by consent and compromise which is nowadays used in certain countries—France, for example.

True, not everything in totalitarianism or in current indifference toward political freedom can be accounted for through the consideration of the new trends which affect our societies geared toward greater complexity. Still, totalitarian enterprises have much in common with the new social techniques of propaganda, mass-media manipulation, and efficient bureaucratic administration. According to some observers, it is the progress of technology and, characteristically, the progress of social technology which made possible in our times a hitherto-unknown brand of totalitarian dictatorship. "Totalitarian dictatorship," say C. J. Friedrich and Z. K. Brzezinski, "is historically unique and *sui generis.*" [2] According to them, it is precisely unique because of the new possibilities offered by social technology, by applied social sciences. In former autocracies "the limits of technology prevented a fully consequent development of totalitarianism." In the newer societies total political control by political terror "systematically exploited modern science

[2] *Totalitarian Dictatorship and Autocracy*, Cambridge: Harvard University Press, 1956, p. 5.

and, more especially, scientific psychology." [3] The monopoly of the means of mass communication is again made possible by modern technology. The bureaucratic organization of modern dictatorship is served by new technological devices.

Another aspect of totalitarian constructions is a "centrally directed economy," which presupposes "transmission, registration, and tabulation techniques offered by modern technology." All this has transpired in such a way that the totalitarian mode has become characteristic of modern society, to the extent of becoming an endemic disease of our social condition of life. "Totalitarian dictatorship," write Friedrich and Brzezinski, "a novel form of autocracy, more inimical to human dignity than autocracies in the past, appears to be a highly dynamic form of government which is still in the process of evolving. Whether it will, in the long run, prove to be a viable form of social and political organization remains to be seen. Nonetheless, large portions of mankind may have to pass through its crucible before becoming ready, if they survive the ordeal, for more complex forms of political organization." [4] There would be thus at least a time lag between the appearance of all signs of a complex society and the setting up of a correspondingly complex form of government.

At any rate, even where there can be no talk of totalitarianism proper, we are all aware of the relationship between obstacles to initiative and free judgment and the growing complexity of our societies.

Still, after thus allowing for all factors of indifference toward freedom and hesitation about freedom, the other side of the coin must also be shown. It is indeed within the reach of anyone's experience that more complex societies offer many new opportunities for freedom. Not only does such complexity normally accompany wealth and prosperity of nations, which are often an instrument for the expression of freedom, but, still more, complexity as

[3] *Op. cit.*, p. 10.
[4] *Op. cit.*, p. 303.

such, the multiplication and diversification of social bonds, is capable of limiting the influence of any particular allegiance, the degree of coercion of any particular bond. Man may at times be a cog in the factory or in some bureaucratic organization; still he is at the same time a citizen, a member of many communal and cultural associations. He may enjoy communication with a number of fellow men and with a number of communities through the various mass media at hand. Pluralism in participation or allegiance is one of the major opportunities offered by complex societies, compared with traditional simple societies, where one's entire life and activity were channeled by a single social pattern of thought and action.

In order to understand this better, one has but to think of the benefits which the village African or the Indian from the Andean *altiplano* derives from his migration to the cities, even if he has to live there in hard conditions and dwell in miserable shacks. At the end of the nineteenth century Lenin similarly emphasized the benefits deriving for Russian peasants from the intrusion of modern capitalist economy into their village life. It saved them, according to Lenin, from a brutish, uncultivated life; it brought them in contact with a number of other men; it fostered and satisfied their curiosity. To Lenin, according to his own Marxist interpretation, this was a first step toward a consciousness required for revolutionary enterprises. Lately, at another step of development, rural Europe, and particularly rural France, has been benefiting of the same advantages through a new and sudden progress of industrialization in agriculture, after World War II: one of the most surprising and important phenomena of social and political history of those countries since 1950.

Open and plural social life is thus a generally acknowledged benefit. Mobility is again a benefit: local mobility of the individuals—thanks to improved transportation means—mobility within the professional life of men who can change jobs (and often are compelled to do so at some stage of their career), most important of all, mobility of the mind, made possible by the easier communication of ideas. There was probably no deeper revolution in the African bush through the last decade than the rapid spreading of transistor radio. Mobility has its drawbacks, of course, but on the whole it is a rather progressive factor for culture and even for social attitudes.

Thus the opportunities for freedom are many. Lightly regarded by those who have already been enjoying such opportunities for a long time, they are best understood by those who are precisely being newly affected by the transformation from traditional village or tribal life into a more complex industrial, urban, and cultivated social life. A British writer said about Africa that only the European and the African who thinks according to European patterns are likely to lament the ruin of traditional society, whereas the African himself is more keenly aware of the advantages which he is reaping through the process of change. Along with some exaggeration, there is much truth in such conclusion. The degree of satisfaction offered by transition into complex societies may even be the cause for a certain disregard for and indifference to political liberty as such during the first phase of the social transformation.

Pope John XXIII, in his encyclical *Mater et Magistra*, was aware of all such benefits from complex socialized life. "Unquestionably," he said, "many advantages derive from this development in the pattern of living. It can lead to the satisfaction of many human rights, especially in the economic and social sphere. These concern the essentials of life, care of health, broadening and deepening of basic education, fitting preparation for a trade, housing, work, suitable recreation, and the rest" (Number 61). According to him, it is again a great advantage for the person to be able, thanks to mass media, to communicate ideas or feelings with all sorts of people throughout the world.

Still, we cannot be satisfied with so simple an account of the possibilities of freedom in societies of growing complexity. So far we have not given any definition of freedom; we have simply assumed that a certain number of basic aspirations of men toward greater autonomy of the individual, toward communication and mobility, pertain to freedom. But we may also have to revise our conception of freedom on the threshold of socialization, in order to take significant advantage of the new opportunities offered to freedom. We have to discover, for instance, that the definition of freedom as free will or autonomy is too narrow and even falls short of the aim which is implied in the most basic aspirations of men. Free will is conflicting with determinisms, and determinisms are increasing daily; artificial and social determinisms are taking the place of mere natural determinisms. The result is the not-uncommon opinion that man, after all, is not free, or that freedom is only an illusion. In our time, indeed, there is not only practical indifference to freedom, but there is also, very often, a theoretical doubt and skepticism concerning the very fact of man's freedom.

On the other hand, full autonomy, implied in the common definition of freedom, appears as an impossible goal. One or two centuries ago there were men who tried to set up schemes of political life based upon full autonomy of the individual, a difficult, indeed impossible, enterprise. They conceived of freedom as a kind of well-established possession in the hands of the individual, who should not surrender it in any degree. The principle made society and government unnecessary, or at least hardly justifiable. A philosopher such as Rousseau tried to reconcile full autonomy and true society: man would follow and obey his own will through obeying a general will which would be the direct expression of reason, abstracted from all passions and from all interests of particular individuals or of particular groups.

But Rousseau, too, failed in his enterprise (or at least he seemed to fail, if freedom is merely autonomy in the afore-mentioned meaning). He failed in two ways. First, because he admitted a practical incapacity among men at large to rid themselves from all interests and passions: "In order to discover the best rules of society for nations, a superior intelligence would be needed that would see all passions of man without being subject to any one of them; that would not have any relationship to our nature but still would know it perfectly; whose happiness would be independent from ours but who still would take care of our own happiness . . . gods would be needed to give laws to men." [5] Short of gods, a "legislator" is needed. Heteronomy thus creeps in again. On the other hand, even in theory, the device provided, or rather imagined, by Rousseau is hardly satisfactory for reconciling autonomy and society. "Each of us", he said, "puts in common his own person and his own power under the supreme direction of the general will, and we shall also receive each member as an indivisible part of the whole." [6] Clearly enough, it is only through giving up oneself entirely, one's person and one's possessions, that one can enter the society ruled by the general will and reason.

As long as one understands freedom merely as free will and autonomy, there will be a never-ending conflict between freedom and society, social determinisms, social powers. Such a conflict has long been illustrated in the dramatic tension between individual and society in various sectors of liberal thought. Alain, a "radical" thinker in France, could not think of the citizen but as of the "anti-power" (anti-pouvoir).

But liberalism is a too shallow philosophy of freedom, and we can no longer be satisfied with it. Certainly we discover man, or, rather, man discovers himself as a being capable of self-determination (and this implies the concept of free will); this can never be given away. But, for the same reason precisely, we cannot conceive of man as a being already made, as a full-grown, stabilized, and terminated being; and we cannot conceive of freedom as a possession, of free man as a being possessing himself as an asset. He is rather a being capable of determining himself, that is, of becoming what he "is," of making himself, according to the old saying, "Become what thou art." Again, man is man in so far as he

[5] Contrat social, II, c. 6, 7.
[6] Ibid., I, c, 6.

constantly surpasses or transcends himself, his interests, and the determinations which are characteristic of him at a given moment. This really is self-determination: in other words, self-determination is not only the *form* of man's life and activity, a quality added to a being already in full and definitive possession of himself (or without any capacity of transcending himself). Self-determination is also the *content*—or, rather, it has a content. Self-determination, or freedom, is indeed the *aim* which is pursued (and must be pursued) by man determining himself. Freedom can be acquired or aimed at only freely: but free determination is not yet freedom if it does not aim beyond the given or present characteristics of the self-determining being. Thus the affirmation of freedom is not the observation and conservation of what I am here and now, as a physical force, a mental capacity, a property of some kind or other. The affirmation of freedom is rather that of a capacity of transcending oneself. Such a capacity is inherent in man's experience.

From this line of thought there follows first a conclusion with regard to social determinisms which surround us. Freedom does not principally consist in escaping social determinisms, which, after all, are the fruit of past actions of men laboring toward self-determination, toward realization of themselves. Freedom rather consists in the assumption of such given determinisms for the sake of new processes of self-determination. Freedom is not just the "conscience of necessity," according to Hegel's and Marx's words, popularized and probably simplified, too, by Engels and other post-Marxian materialists; otherwise the word "conscience" has to be taken in a very broad and comprehensive meaning. Freedom is thus self-determination within necessity, since there is and never has been any freedom of man—who is not an absolutely free being—outside that field of necessity. When social necessity of determinisms take the place of natural determinisms, there is but a change in the form of determinisms, no fundamental change in man's capacity for self-determination. Still the situation is renewed in the sense that freedom now displays itself in an already humanized nature, in the dimension of history rather than of mere nature.

On this point the answer of Pope John XXIII is again clear and definite. "Shall we say," he asked, "that men, caught up in this increasingly more complicated network, will be progressively entangled and paralyzed and will abdicate their freedom? The answer is: 'No.' " [7] He says further: "The truth of the matter is that the multiplication of social relationships is not brought about by the blind pressure of natural forces." [8] And again: "The development [of interdependency] seems to be due to several features of our times, among which are scientific and technical progress, improvements in industrial efficiency, and a higher standard of living. . . . This development is also a sign and a consequence of a *natural* tendency which can scarcely be restrained: the inclination which moves men spontaneously to enter association with others so that they might be able to obtain results which each would like to have, but to which none of his single efforts could attain." [9] A "natural inclination" of man, therefore: how could such a natural tendency of man (toward a more socialized life) be contrary to fundamental human freedom? "As we have already pointed out," says John XXIII, "the multiplication of social relationships is the creation of men who have freedom to choose, whose nature impels them to activity, and who must accept the consequences of their actions." [10] Even where they become deeply involved in social life or social construction, men never lose their responsibility or their capacity for new free responses. True, according to the Pope, "they must acknowledge the laws of human progress and the course of economic development and be, as it were, obedient to them: they cannot altogether ignore the strength of external influences." Still all this is man's own work, man's past, the fruit of his own activity,

[7] Number 62.
[8] *Mater et Magistra*, Number 63.
[9] Number 60.
[10] Number 63.

of his efforts in order to realize his own self; and he does not lose the capacity of renewing his world over and over again on the basis of existing determinisms.

If absolute autonomy cannot be expected—it would not be a blessing for man—initiative and responsibility nonetheless have an extreme value for the self-realization of men engaged in a socialized world or in a more complex society. The times call for initiative and responsibility; but above all the more valuable of the two, responsibility, which could be called social freedom, or the constructive exercise of freedom in and through society. As John XXIII said: "The economic order is far removed from justice wherever machines and methods are used which endanger the human dignity of the workers, weaken their sense of responsibility, or take away from them the opportunity to use initiative. This is so even if output be high and its distribution conform to justice and equity." [11] Justice is beyond justice in the common sense of the word; it is realized only through the possible exercise of initiative and responsibility for everyone—that is, through the exercise of freedom in society.

Thus not only does freedom, in the first and elemental sense of the word—of autonomy, the absence of coercion—find new and better opportunities in more complex societies, but even those higher aspects of freedom, initiative, and responsibility (freedom geared toward transcending oneself in the direction of the others' good) find in a denser social life an occasion for manifestation and progress. Never in a simpler context can man be so free as he can in such a dense network of interdependences.

This also means, indeed, that neither man nor his freedom was ever before challenged in such a way as it is today and will be in the future. One must remember, however, that man, since he is man, is under some form of that challenge of freedom—rather than being in possession of freedom as a fixed asset. Of course this should not be taken as an over-optimistic statement; it by no means dispels the

[11] *Mater et Magistra*, Number 83.

anxiety and fears which are natural when one considers the totalitarian possibilities in modern technology, especially social and psychological technology, manipulation, and bureaucratic techniques. Our contention is, rather, that such perils are enhanced by each progress of society and of complexity in society. Never has man indeed—either individually or collectively—made any progress without accepting new perils. In other words, the possibilities of freedom are at their greatest where precisely the threats to freedom are also most numerous and menacing.

A few years ago Teilhard de Chardin was considering the modification of our societies, "socialization" as he already termed it, as a new step in the process of evolution. Complexity, or rather complexification, even in the biological sphere, appeared to him to be the law of progress: no mind can appear but on the ground of such complexification of the body to the extreme degree of delicacy and frailty. Man is the weakest of all animals. The law of complexity, Teilhard contended, still applies to man and to his history. But the expression of this law is no longer to be expected in the field of corporal arrangement of man. It now takes place through the means of a process of socialization, of growing interdependence, and of a move toward unity between the various members of mankind. Socialization is by God's grace, in the mystical Body of Christ.

Of course no termination can be assigned; but the present process is not a mere accident, it is not a mere external circumstance to be coped with by common means at hand. "We imagine," says Teilhard, "that we are just going through a storm, whereas we are really entering a new climate. If one wants to see in socialization only a haphazard arrangement, a *modus vivendi* without any worth of internal growth, then everything in the world becomes artificial, everything loses gravity, urgency, even interest." [12] In other words, as free beings we cannot escape discovering a profound human

[12] *Avenir de l'homme*, 324.

meaning in a process like socialization, which is the fruit of human liberty aiming at the realization of liberty. If socialization were just an accident, a kind of natural event, then it would mean that our freedom remains a mere form without content, or that it has practically no empirical existence. Our actual lives, our history would be meaningless.

Socialization, therefore, has to be taken up very seriously as an *event for freedom*; but also, as we said, as a challenge to freedom. As a matter of fact, any event for freedom is a challenge to freedom. This is why in the time of greatest opportunities for freedom nothing is ever gained or secured but by active freedom itself. The greatest dangers lie ahead of us. Challenged mankind may refuse to answer. This would lead to the worst of situations: "termite hill instead of brotherhood," said Teilhard. Teilhard was also of the view that history cannot end with such a failure—or else it would lose its meaning. Speaking of totalitarian regimes, he said: "Before such a deep perversion of the rules of the Noogenesis I think that our reaction must not be despair but re-examination. . . . Is not modern totalitarianism, monstrous as it may be, only a deformation of a most magnificent thing? Is it not thus quite close to the truth?" [13]

In other words, mankind will live up to the goal of its destiny—that is, live up to the ideal of self-determination and freedom—only if it takes up the challenge, not through denying or trying to escape it. Again, freedom can exist today only if it is consciously achieved. We have to re-examine ourselves and to adopt new attitudes, to set up new social devices in order to live free in a society which is capable of the grossest threats to freedom.

Pope John XXIII concludes his remarks on the growing interdependence of men with two pieces of advice. The first precisely conveys the necessity of a higher *consciousness* of the social good.

[13] *Le Phénomène humain,* 285.

He simply says: "This desirable purpose [of avoiding or reducing the inconveniences of socialization] will be more easily attained if those in charge of public affairs have a correct idea of the common good." [14] And we all know that many people influence public affairs within any complex society, not only in an official democracy but even in a complex society not yet organized as one.

The second admonition of Pope John is to the effect that we should not refrain from engaging in the numerous new social bonds that are offered to us. At the same time we should find devices in order to bring humanity and freedom into social constructions themselves. We consider it to be necessary that the vocational groups or associations and other manifold organizations—it is these which form the chief strands in the developing web of social relationships—should be truly self-governing and pursue their ends in the mutual harmony and with regard for the common good. It is no less necessary for societies of this kind to exhibit the characteristics of a community. This they will do to the extent that their members are treated always as persons and are called to play their part in the management of affairs." [15]

We have isolated, then, the two main conditions for freedom in societies of growing complexity. First, there is the necessity for true self-government in the decentralized social bodies which make up a great society. Second, there is the equal necessity of a personal participation of each member within each body, each social network, each organization. One must participate with full responsibility and let others participate with full initiative. These are some of the main aspects of the social ethics required by socialization, if man is to take advantage of the possibilities for freedom in tomorrow's complex societies.

[14] *Mater et Magistra*, Number 65.
[15] *Mater et Magistra*, Number 65.

THE METAPHYSICS OF FREEDOM

CHARLES MALIK

I

The reflections I shall set forth on the topic of freedom, of course, require further elucidation. But they are some of the important conclusions I have so far arrived at in this field. Conclusions of this order of metaphysical ultimacy are literally "summings up," "concludings," "termini" of whole strands of lived and living experience. This is what I have found, this is what I have gathered, this is what I believe, this is what I know from a life of study, reflection, intense experience, and direct vision. In an order of complete trust it would perhaps be sufficient merely to state your conclusions, and people trusting you and sharing with you a whole community of love and being would at once understand what you mean, and would perhaps believe you, thus relieving you of any necessity of discursive elaboration; vision then passes immediately from mind to mind. The enunciation of simple, declarative aphorisms would be the norm of communication in such an order.

Part of the wisdom of the East is precisely to dispense with all argument and to state at once your conclusions in pithy aphorisms or what are called proverbs and sayings, and trustingly to leave it at that; and in the deepest instances even sayings are dispensed with in favor of the fullness of being. It is not so much by talking as by living that the sage teaches; in fact, he is not teaching at all, he simply is, and his being itself infects and overflows. I never cease to wonder at the astounding fact, which judges and in a sense con-

demns all talk, certainly every written word, that the three men
who influenced history more than any other three men, namely,
Socrates, Jesus, and Muhammad, never wrote a single word. And in
Christian faith this debunking of the verbal argument is expressed
by the doctrine of the Incarnation, namely, that the eternal Word
in whom the wisdom of God dwelleth wholly and bodily, nay, who
is himself the Wisdom of God, and by whom all things were made,
including, of course, words and reason and argument, took on flesh
and blood "and dwelt among us, full of grace and truth."

In an order of complete trust conclusions are enough. This is the
order of people who know and trust and love one another; this is
the order between parents and children and between teachers and
pupils where the parents and teachers are responsible and the
children and pupils not rebellious; and whether or not it is one of
complete trust, this is the implicit order of military command. The
satisfaction of the East for the most part with unargued aphorisms
stems from the East's infinite yearning for heaven, for it is in
heaven alone that you do not reason or argue: in heaven you only
see. And while its neglect of earth, of the whole realm of means,
has inflicted upon it endless earthly penalties, its unfeigned love of
heaven has recompensed it here and there, by heaven itself having
pity on it, with wonderful visions, and in the case of Christ, with
the eternal Logos Himself, the very fullness of heaven itself, first
appearing on earth in its midst.

Together with heaven, the realm of God and ultimate ends, the
West is preoccupied at the same time with earth, the whole realm
of what Aristotle would call "proximate causes," and at its best
throughout the ages the West was faithful to both realms. Deca-
dence sets in as soon as proximate causes overwhelm and displace
final ends. To lose sight of the proximate, or to be so lost in it as to
lose sight of the ultimate, or again to place the two rationalistically
on the same plane, any one of these three possibilities expresses a
curse, a judgment, a condemnation. The maintenance of the right

order and subordination between the two are a grace which, again to revert to the wisdom of the East, only God can dispense.

We are not in heaven where vision is sufficient and where there is immediate communication without argument and without elaboration. I cannot assume that there is between us an order of complete trust in which you will believe me as soon as I utter my conclusions on the subject of freedom. You rightly demand that I argue, that I prove my positions. The incredible insistence in the Bible on every page on belief, belief, belief is so maddening that at some point it will suddenly open your eyes to the fact that belief and believing are the most important things in life.

Man is fundamentally plagued both with unbelief and disbelief: he must be convinced. And let no one imagine that conviction is something mechanical or automatic, not even as a result of the use of the most watertight rational argument. Nothing convinces the rebellious, not even sheer force if he has made up his mind to die in disbelief; and there is such a thing as the will to radical rebellion. There is an ultimate grace which independently must come in even to be convinced of the most rational of arguments. The will to believe, the active readiness to be convinced, the pure heart, must be there from the beginning prior to all argument and all reasoning. That is why some sages never wasted their time arguing with the unconvincible; and that is why, in the case of Christ, far from wasting any time on this type of mind, He often provoked it intentionally to maximum disbelief and rebellion.

But if we are not in heaven, neither are we on earth only. I can, I think, assume a certain amount of trust which will justify my stating some of my conclusions without proof. I can point to direct visions, leaving it, completely trustingly on my part, to whoever attends to them to work back their ground and their justification. I think there is enough of heaven around to justify this procedure.

But both because I am talking here on earth, because the freedom I am talking about is, at least in part, freedom here on earth, and because I am certainly fallible, I must argue my positions as best I can. Reason is an absolute necessity on earth, but in heaven we "see face to face." Reason, therefore, is ordered to our imperfect earthly condition; it is, therefore, at once a curse and a glory: a curse and a tedium in so far as it measures and reflects the imperfection of our human condition, but the greatest possible glory because it fits perfectly this condition such as it is.

My presentation is therefore mixed. There is some proof but there is not enough of it. The determination of the proportions of the two ingredients in this mixture characterizes the person himself: his limitations of time, his limitations of circumstance, his limitations of competence, his sense of humor, the way his mind works, and the like. On top of all this it is always also a question of free personal decision.

II

Whitehead coined the phrase "the metaphysical situation." He meant by it the few ultimate convictions of the philosopher beyond which he cannot go, and on the basis of which, and within which, and between which, his thought navigates: in a word, his ultimate vision, his first principles. He often chides philosophers for "slipping in" assumptions in the course of their argument; he wants them, as it were, to put all their cards on the table from the start. There are dangers, both methodological and substantive, in this procedure. Despite these dangers, however, I shall employ it in the present instance.

I live and think and talk, without any apology whatsoever, on the basis of and within the following ultimate convictions:

1. God exists. He is not the god of Whitehead or of the philosophers but the God of Abraham, Isaac, and Jacob, who is also identically He whom Jesus Christ called His Father. He creates and has created everything out of nothing; therefore everything is ultimately upheld by Him.

2. Nothing comes from nothing. Things have not arisen from the darkness of time, from the impenetrable abyss of the past, from nowhere. All this is magic. The world or any part of it is wholly impotent to create or sustain itself. Beings have all come from the fullness of being which is God. He created them from nothing, but He is prior to them and to nothing.

3. There are many wonderful traditions outside the Judaeo-Christian tradition, but this tradition is most unique. It understands and judges all other traditions far better than they understand and judge it, and the understander occupies a distinguished ontological position with respect to the understood.

4. It follows that the Church, which embodies and conserves the Judaeo-Christian tradition, is a unique historical organization. Since it exists mightily and has existed for centuries, since it claims that it has a unique relationship to God and Christ, and since this claim has been believed and is believed by countless human beings, its findings and pronouncements on man and his freedom cannot be overlooked by any serious student seeking to gather all the evidence on the subject.

5. It follows, further, that the Bible, being *the* Book of the Church, is the most important book in existence. Its findings on man and his freedom must therefore be taken most seriously.

6. Man, namely, you and I in the first person, is given by God his Creator some of God's own powers; that is, to understand, to create, to love, and to dominate. He has these powers, however, only as a creature. Moreover, for some reason man has abused this gift. It was on account of this abuse that God from His compassion for man intervened in Jesus Christ in order to restore man to Himself.

7. Just as man, namely, you and I in the first person, owes everything to God, so God is his only final end.

8. Pride, which can take the form of false humility, inordinate ambition, vested interests, callousness, arrogance, self-sufficiency, hatred, selfishness, rebellion by the lower against the higher, and

the worship of something, including perhaps oneself, other than God, is the ultimate cause of all evil and suffering in the world.

9. Reason is man's natural glory. By it we argue and communicate and understand each other; by it we penetrate and understand the vast creation of God; by it we understand our own limitations; and it can point to God from a distance, but it cannot do much more. Thus the embodiments of reason in the sciences and the arts, and in the diverse cultural creations of man, are real graspings of the objective, given truth.

10. The positive tradition of thought, from Pythagoras and Socrates to Hegel and Whitehead, despite its incredible diversity and its many inner contradictions, abberations, and abstractions, constitutes, as to its continuity, richness, thickness, comprehensiveness, historical efficacy, and relevance, and internal self-reflection and self-verification, the greatest unity of thought in existence. It has, as Hegel said, a hidden music of its own, although it may not be quite the melody he himself heard. When this unity of thought coalesces with the Judaeo-Christian tradition we have something incomparably wonderful.

11. The importance of Aristotle, both in history and for the present historical moment, is that for centuries in the Middle Ages he more than any other man brought East and West together. He constitutes a common language and a common world of thought between Christianity and Islam. The only modern example of a single thinker who brought East and West together in this sense on an even larger scale is Marx.

12. Nothing is as valuable for the understanding of man and his freedom as the saints, especially the philosopher saints.

13. There is a real, existing, independent realm of values or essences wholly accessible to the human mind. This realm of values includes such things as friendship, honesty, love, justice, self-sacrifice, integrity, purity; in fact, all the Platonic ideas. The weakness of Plato and all idealists since had been in their being equivocal about the precise relationship between God and the ideas. The

ideas, the essences, the values are not side by side with God; from Him alone they obtain their essence and in Him alone they exist.

14. There is a given hierarchy of being completely undefinable except through itself. If you do not see it, you do not know it, and if you do not know it, you can never suspect or deduce its existence. The propositions: "A free man is better or higher than a slave"; "the understanding subject is better or higher than the understood object"; "the Creator is better or higher than the creature"; "man is better or higher than the animal"; "life is better or higher than lifeless things"; "being is better or higher than not-being"; all these propositions can be analyzed, explained, expounded in a thousand-and-one ways; but always in the end unless the ultimate ontological hierarchy reveals itself to you and you see it, you miss the central point. The fullness of being which is God is the apex and source of the hierarchy.

15. History is most real, for in it man is tested by God. Whether our decisions affect our personal destiny alone, or whether, if we are politically or socially or intellectually responsible, they affect also the destiny of others, including at times the destiny of whole cultures and whole nations, in all our decisions we are always directly responsible to God, the living God who has actually spoken in history.

16. Although God is behind history, He is also "beyond" it. If our end were only in history we would be most miserable, because certainly one day we are going to die and vanish. Our end is in God who is "beyond" history. The dimension of "the beyond" is closed to modern man, and that is his fundamental agony.

17. Man's achievements in history—his diverse cultures, creations, certainties—are all honorable and respectable. None of them is without its inherent truth. They are all entitled to the utmost respect. But they are mixed with error and they all decay. Thus their validity is only relative. There is genuine, abiding being beyond all culture, all earthly loyalties. Friendship, class, party, nation, culture—all these things are nothing compared to the

fullness of being which is God, on which all these things ultimately depend.

18. Suffering is the only path to real being. But there is hopeful suffering and there is hopeless suffering. Without hopeful voluntary suffering, blessedness is impossible.

This is my "metaphysical situation." From its soil I interpret man and his freedom. I have placed all my cards on the table, and so there is no possibility now of my playing any trick by "slipping in" anything new. Thus it is not a subjective theory I am urging or a favorite "system" I wish to gloat over. I endeavor to listen to the music of the ages. It appears something eclectic, but it is not different from the eclecticism of the Bible, or indeed of Aristotle. Adequacy is higher than consistency, affirms Whitehead, and one can only be adequate by complete openness to being. And since being, as Aristotle declares, is not a genus, complete openness to it can only be the thankful submission to being, however and wherever, it reveals itself. This is that healthy eclecticism which is adequate to the total evidence. It is the conscious repudiation of that false "autonomy of reason" whereby one willfully imposes upon being one's idea and one's notion. The open perspective of being is the real thing, not the perspective of the individual philosopher. Let being, then, itself speak.

III

Cosmological freedom, freedom "in the universe," is a false notion. When Bergson affirms freedom in evolution or Whitehead freedom in "far-off empty space" or in the "occasions of experience" in this table or even in his own brain, they are only projecting their own sense of freedom upon something they really know nothing about. This is not a phenomenon in the phenomenological sense of the term, but a speculation. They "were" never "there," neither "in evolution" when "it occurred," nor in the table or the brain, nor certainly in "far-off empty space," to be sure that what they were talking about was true; it is only a penchant of their mind. It is a theoretical construction of a mind trying to establish a monistic system over "the entire universe." The prior question, therefore, is why this particular mind chose the road of monistic construction. Cosmological freedom, then, becomes a personal question about the cosmologist himself. It has no ontological validity.

Nor can we conclude anything about "freedom in the atom" from quantum mechanics and the doctrine of indeterminacy. All we can properly say here is that we are before certain experimental effects which can make sense, at least for the time being, only on the assumption of certain discontinuous equations descriptive of time and space. Bridgman's operationalism, which appears to me to be an exact phenomenological account of the process of physical experimentation, precludes the possibility of "transferring freedom" to the atom. From beginning to end we are shut up within human sensible observation. Nothing about "the universe in itself" can be concluded from this.

Kant was on much sounder ground when he affirmed freedom only of man. The facts of his moral life—responsibility, choice, punishment, guilt, anguish—prove it. At any moment alternatives present themselves from among which we choose either blindly and haphazardly, or in accordance with previously determined, or chosen ends which they serve. Responsibility clings both to the choice of the ends and the means. Only as man is presented with genuine alternatives, and only as he has the real power of throwing himself upon one and destroying the others, in full knowledge of what he is doing, and only as he then stands up for his choice and accepts full accountability for it, for good or for ill, including even the danger of his death, is man free and therefore is he man. Man "is himself" only in freedom, namely, in being able truthfully to say that the situation in which he finds himself is his own free choice, for the consequences of which he assumes full responsibility.

In the end man is always responsible and always free. The proof of this is that he can commit suicide. The possibility of suicide is the rock-bottom proof of the reality of freedom. No man can plead for any situation that he had no alternative, for it can always be pointed out to him that at least he could have committed suicide. He chose that possibility rather than the destruction of all possibilities through suicide; therefore he was free and responsible. Animals do not commit suicide; in the case of the cornered scorpion, it is always a question whether she "knew" what she was doing; and in any event, it is not the species that commits suicide but that particular individual whose whole *raison d'être* is to serve the species. No species of animals, including man, has ever committed suicide; on the contrary, its most inveterate tendency is to perpetuate itself.

But every human is a sort of species unto himself; this is the meaning of the Christian doctrine that he has an immortal soul; he has a distinctive name, whereas no animal has such a name, except insofar as man projects one upon it. Buber's I-and-thou situation does not apply to animals: they are all "its." And no man who commits suicide "does not know what he is doing." The very possibility of man committing suicide, or risking his life in obedience to some "heavenly vision," as in the case of Antigone or the martyrs, proves unmistakably the freedom of man. A slave certainly has the two alternatives either of risking his life by defying his oppressors or at the very least of committing suicide. When at least one of these alternatives is not open to him, he is no longer man; and some, alas, do sink to the level of the subhuman. No man is ever forced not to commit suicide. If he is, he ceases to be human. Therefore for any man who denies his own freedom, the answer is: But, my friend, you certainly can jump from that window!

IV

This is an age of group freedom. The individual human is relatively in eclipse. Groups want to be free, want to be themselves, but not individual persons. The individual person is assimilated to his group. His group is more real, more ultimate than he. The group could be a nation or a class or a party or a race or a culture, and when the five merge into one, as in the case of China, there is a most formidable group determinism. Thus one is American or German or Asian or communist or colored or white. The nationalist, the socialist, the racist thinks as his respective group expects him to: he surrenders his personal freedom to the freedom of his group. When you talk to him you do not feel you are talking to a free man; the whole notion of "a free man" is anathema to him. He is not "a free man," he is "a group man." You distinctly feel he is in the clutch of something, he is being held back by something. When he talks to you in the presence of members of his party you notice a subtle competition between them as to who could be more extreme; but even when you talk to him alone, you observe that they are present, too. He is never alone, not even in their absence. He always has at the back of his mind, and sometimes at the side of his mind, what his nation or his class or his party or his race or his culture expects from him. He is determined by it.

The classical modern description of this state of being is Heidegger's *das Man*. Individual, personal freedom, involving laughing at himself and his group, seeing them in the light of alternatives, criticizing them, detaching himself from them, defying them, being himself over against being them, measuring them by something "higher" and "better," being loyal to something "above" them and "beyond" them, transcending them to the extent of loving and respecting other groups as much as his own, indeed sending them to hell if necessary—all this is impossible to the group man. He cannot stand being alone; he cannot bear his personal freedom; he finds it, as Dostoyevsky would say, too heavy a burden to bear. Consequently, he surrenders it at the feet of the first group he finds himself belonging to; he then becomes the adherent of a "cause" which relieves him of himself; he thus acquires warmth and security; he is no longer a "thou." What is immortal now is no longer his soul but the group to which he belongs. He willingly sacrifices himself to secure its immortality.

Modern existentialism, from Kierkegaard to Heidegger and Sartre, is a revolt against group freedom. Not the universal but the particular, not the group but the individual human, is the real thing. Freedom resides in the decision of each existing individual. If there is immortality, he alone is immortal, not the group. Modern existentialism recaptures the freedom of the individual human soul for the most part without God. That is why it ends in despair, absurdity, and nothingness, the very despair in which ancient stoicism ended when Christianity appeared on the scene to save the world. It is not the jump into nothingness that liberates us, it is the jump into the fullness of being. When Sartre affirms: "You create yourself," he is right in enthroning freedom back in the individual human soul over against any group compulsion; but he is absurd in meaning that you literally create yourself. Yet he does not mind absurdity; in fact, he revels in it. And incidentally he raises the problem of creation and origins, the most ultimate problem in philosophy; but with his presuppositions he can never solve it. If he is free, what are the origins of his freedom? Simply nothing? That question he can never face, let alone answer.

The nationalists and the socialists tell you: Assure group freedom—the freedom of the nation and economic and social security and justice—and individual, personal freedom would follow. This is a pious hope. The more you absolutize the group, the less chance the individual human person will have to breathe. Worship the glory and grandeur of your nation, and you will forget about yourself as a deciding individual person. Seek first economic and social security, and you will be enslaved by the endless seductions of desire. Thus what the nationalists and socialists really mean when they tell you: Assure group freedom and personal freedom will follow, is that they do not really care for personal freedom. In their scale of values they place group freedom above personal freedom; if seeking the first should mean the atrophy of the second, they do not mind. They pay lip service to personal freedom so as to silence those who still care for it, and when these have all perished, they will cease talking about personal freedom altogether.

There are genuine emergencies when group freedom suspends many an individual freedom. Such an emergency is war. But in such cases the memory of freedom will survive the suspension, both in literature, in law, in the institutions of freedom, such as the church, the university, the home, and the economic enterprise, and in the mind of living persons. Where no memory of pre-existing freedom survives, group freedom cannot create individual freedom from nothing. Thus when the new countries and cultures which are seeking group freedom assure the world that personal freedom will follow, the world has every right to answer: Since we do not believe in creation *ex nihilo* by man, show us first vestiges of freedom in your own culture, whether in literature or in law or in institutions or in individual men, before we can trust that when you have perfected your group freedom, personal freedom will follow.

Only where personal freedom exists, at least in germ, side by side with group freedom, and indeed as the end and *raison d'être* of the latter, can there be any justified hope that personal freedom will come into being, let alone flourish, when group freedom is in full sway. And in the extreme cases where no trace or vestige or memory of personal freedom exists, personal freedom must invade the area in question from the outside before man can be free. Existing freedom alone generates freedom.

V

Surely in existing authentically I am most free when I am myself, when I can stand being alone without rebelling, when I am an individual over against the whole world, realizing my own possibilities, no matter how limited, including the greatest limitation of all, namely, my death. Authentic existence in the Heideggerian sense is itself freedom.

But this existence, this freedom, is impossible without God. This is Heidegger's weakness. He does not raise the radical question of origins. He discriminates and describes authentic and unauthentic existence, but *how to be* authentic over against unauthentic existence he never tells us. To say this is not the task of the philosopher may satisfy the speculative but certainly not the existential philosopher. Heidegger simply "finds" that *we are* these two possibilities of being, and up to this point he is perfectly right. But how to be the one *rather than* the other is a sort of miracle for him. We simply exist authentically *and* unauthentically—that is all.

But to the poor heart that thirsts for being, that is not all; the heart that pants after being wants to be, and the most superb phenomenological description will only whet its desire: it will not alone enable it to be. Such a heart *knows* that life is worthless without the moments, few and far between as they may be, of authentic existence. It wants these moments at any price. It is not comforted by the phenomenological assurance that while life may be these moments it is also the moments of gossip, curiosity, self-forgetfulness, and self-lostness in things. Its authentic existence is its supreme being, and it loathes the other moments of its life for its sake. This "wanting" the supreme at any price, this "loathing" the fallen and ordinary, is as much a phenomenon as the phenomenon that we are both possibilities "at the same time." What is more, it carries with it a craving for the supreme, and in this phenomenon of craving, of the eros, we have implanted in the heart of man a pointer toward God.

Only the actual, independent, genuine, sovereign, free, existing Being of the Supreme can lead man to supreme being. The eros, then, demands and proves God. But it proves much more than that. It proves the necessity of faith and revelation. The Supreme Being must disclose Himself; I am impotent to disclose Him, for who am I to be able to do that? And with His self-disclosure He must also "grant" or "give" or "confer" or "bestow" the power of self-transcendence upon miserable man. Genuinely craving the Supreme, man is unable to rise to supreme being without the active intervention of the Supreme Himself. This is, of course, a miracle, but it is a different one from that of Heidegger. To Heidegger how I am authentic *rather than* unauthentic is a miracle, but to the believer God intervenes. He trusts Him; the miracle here is an attested one.

The defect of phenomenology, great as this movement is, is its satisfaction with description. But being precedes description, even the most perfect description of being itself. Description as an end, even of philosophical perfection, is a sort of self-indulgence; it denatures the soul. For the soul wants simply to be, and it hates simply to be described. The joy of description is nothing compared to the joy of being for the philosopher who supremely and authentically *is*. In the presence of the Supreme, by participating in its being, the philosopher suddenly forgets all his philosophy. And he never regrets it.

A deep tragedy appears to characterize some philosophers, of the Nietzsche or Heidegger type, one whose ultimate secret God alone knows. The craving is pure and unmistakable, but there is always about them the aspect of a man trying to lift himself by his bootstraps. But because they loved much, God is likely to forgive them. Being is interested in itself and not just in being described or craved for. Being is there in its fullness, and it owes me nothing. But I owe my individuality, my freedom, my joy, my supreme being, wholly to it. My freedom comes from the original freedom of God.

VI

There is no freedom without the possibility of rebellion. You must know the truth and be able to reject it to be free. That is why there should be no coercion upon you to espouse it. The espousal must be entirely free, it must be entirely your own. The truth liberates you when, in the face of the possibility of rebelling against it, you nevertheless accept it. Surely it must first reveal itself to you, but in the presence of its self-revelation you can either accept it with thanks or you can reject it. The natural right of man to freedom of thought, conscience, belief, and expression, such as is proclaimed in the Universal Declaration of Human Rights, is grounded in the metaphysical fact that man must be able to rebel and reject the truth to be free.

But from the necessity of the possibility of rebellion to be free, its actuality does not follow. It is enough that you *can* rebel—that constitutes your freedom. It does not follow from this that you *must* rebel to prove your freedom. For if you *must* rebel to prove your freedom, you are no longer free not to rebel. When you do rebel, of course, your action is grounded in the possibility of rebellion; but it is not necessary that you rebel to prove your freedom. Thus when you do rebel it was neither your freedom nor God who created you free that caused you to rebel, but some independent dark power. That is, of course, the devil. The devil is the technical term given throughout the ages to the mystery inherent in the strange metaphysical situation, more or less dimly perceived by virtually all peoples and all cultures, that whereas I must be able to rebel to be free, and while it is not necessary for me actually to rebel to prove this ability, nevertheless I do rebel.

The devil does not prove freedom; the devil uses freedom as an occasion to achieve his own ends. For it must never be forgotten that since you are as much free not to rebel as to rebel, you prove your freedom by not rebelling when you could have rebelled just as much as by rebelling when you could not have rebelled. And knowing the devil, and considering that his supreme pleasure is to lead you more and more into not-being and darkness, you are actually more free when you do not rebel although you could, than when you do rebel, although you could not. The "more" here, of course, is not a quantitative measure: it only means "genuinely free." For then you are free toward being and not toward not-being, and the ontological distinction between being and not-being, and therefore the immediate pursuasion that the one is "better" than the other, is altogether irreducible.

All philosophy, all existence, is a quest of being and not of not-being, but of being with the ever-present danger of slipping back into not-being. We start from this: there is no appeal beyond it, there is no going before or behind it.

But I can go on preaching freedom in this vein until doomsday, and yet the devil will come when I least suspect his coming, and he will whisper and paint and insinuate, and I will rebel and fall to the sweetness and deceitfulness of sin. I then either cry with the Apostle: "Oh, wretched man that I am! Who shall deliver me from the body of this death?" and stop there in disgust and loathing; or I go on to say: "I thank God through Jesus Christ our Lord." Whether my end is loathing or gratitude—this is my ultimate freedom.

But this takes me outside myself altogether: I am now before the grace of God. Sin does not exist so that by it I can prove my freedom; this is sheer rebellion and pride; sin exists in order to humble me and throw me back upon God. And then I begin to understand what Augustine repeats on virtually every page, namely, that God resists the proud but gives grace to the humble.

And the problem of election begins to loom in my mind. Being must communicate itself, for nothing comes from nothing. It is only through God's grace that I am freed from sin and death; therefore, since some never follow Job's wife and curse God no matter what happens to them, there is an ultimate sense, to be fully elucidated, in which being communicates itself freely to whomever it pleases. People call it luck and fortune, but this is no luck at all: it is the hand of God reaching forth, freely, graciously, sovereignly—in the words of Paul—"from the foundation of the world" and "from my mother's womb."

In this state of grace I am "in the spirit." I then love, trust, and hope. Without these three there is no freedom. But love, trust, and hope come only from God. It is the actual, historical outpouring of the Spirit of God in history that has given rise to love, trust, and hope among men.

The free man loves and responds to love. The free man trusts and is trustworthy. The free man is full of hope, because he knows that God has raised and can raise even from the dead. Sin and death are nothing, then, when it comes to the power of God.

We hope because Christ is risen from the dead. We believe this because we trust those who were witnesses of the resurrection. We could neither trust nor hope were it not that we belong to an actual, existing order of love in the Church.

Freedom from sin and the devil—this is our deepest hope. Freedom from decay and death—this is our deepest faith. Freedom for the fullness of being in God—this we understand only in the actual order of love.

And when we are free *from* not-being and free *for* being we taste the four ultimate fruits of freedom: strength, joy, creativity, and peace. The strength of the free man is out of this world; so is his joy; so is his creativity; so, certainly, is his peace.

In God we create like Him, and the simplicity and the directness and the certainty of creation are incredible. In God we experience the strength of the eternal. In God there is the infinite joy of communion. And in God there is the peace which passeth all understanding.

We thus see how the metaphysics of freedom pursued relentlessly takes us in the end outside the realm of metaphysics altogether. For freedom is being, and metaphysics is only its reflection.

ON THE THEOLOGY OF FREEDOM

KARL RAHNER, S.J.

A brief treatment of the theology of freedom must forgo historical survey and extended scriptural exegesis. It must content itself, instead, with, at the most, a synthesis of relevant matter from Revelation. One should note, further, that only very gradually do certain ultimate and indelible aspects of the nature of freedom crystallize in philosophical statement, even though they are lived, before such examination, in every one of our acts and in the course of our personal and collective history. The history of salvation and revelation, which includes the history of Christian theology, is thus a history as well of man's philosophical examination of himself as a free being. This is not to say that man always knows with adequate explicitness what human freedom is, nor, on the other hand, to deny that he alters and deepens his concept of freedom when he uses the language of revelation and theology to express it. For the history of revelation is also essentially the history of man's coming to his full heritage as man—and therefore it is the history of his freedom. This freedom, moreover, is a natural reality pre-existing the history of man's reception of it.

In Jesus Christ the history of salvation has arrived at its definitive and unsurpassable eschatological state. The fact that there can now be no going beyond this position in the context of our world history cannot be taken as an arbitrary disposition by God, as if He simply does not wish to reveal any more to us. It must be, rather, something in the very nature of this eschatological condition, to be, by definition, surpassed now only by the immediate vision of God.

When we reach the highest point of revelation in Christ, we reach
at the same time the highest point of the self-realization of human
freedom. Freedom, understood as communicated to man by God in
permanent creation, is freedom to accept absolutely the absolute
mystery we call God. We engage in this acceptance in such a way
that God is not merely one of the objects for which we have, along
with others, some neutral freedom of choice. On the contrary, God
is rather the one who "dawns on" man, first of all in this absolute
act of freedom, and in whom alone the nature of freedom itself
comes to its complete realization.

Freedom in the theological sense is freedom that derives from
and is directed toward God. It would be a complete misapprehen-
sion of the nature of freedom if one were to regard it as the mere
capacity to choose between individual objects given *a posteriori*,
among which God would then be placed along with many others.
It would be equally fallacious if one were to hold that God, among
these objects, plays a special role in the actual choice made by this
freedom only because of His own peculiar nature and not because
of the nature of freedom itself. Freedom is possible only because
there is spirit as transcendence; this point is explicit in St. Thomas.
Unlimited transcendence to being as such and, hence, indifference
in regard to any particular finite object within the context of this
absolute transcendence are to be found only in such a way that this
transcendence, in every particular act concerned with a finite object, is always related to the basic unity of being as such: that is, to
God.

Further, this is so only in so far as this act of transcendence—
which is the basis of every categorial relation to a finite object and,
for that matter, to the infinite, too, in relation to finite concepts—
is supported by a permanent self-disclosure and self-presentation of
the context of this transcendence. In other words, freedom has a
theological character, not under a concept regarding God explicitly
in terms of categorial objectivity along with other objects, but
always as part of the nature of freedom itself. God is to be found,

unreflected on, in every act of freedom, as its supporting ground and ultimate term. When St. Thomas says that God is known in every object and not in a reflective way but nonetheless really, this surely applies equally to the case of freedom. God is willed in every act of freedom, not in a reflective way but nonetheless really. Conversely, it is only in this way that we experience what is really meant by God: the term, beyond the reach of mind and heart and therefore essentially mystery, of the single basic transcendence of man which is analyzable into knowledge and love.

What is decisive for the Christian understanding of freedom, however, is not that this freedom is empowered by God and related to Him as the supporting context of categorial freedom of choice, but that freedom, in a sense, withstands God. This is the terrifying mystery of freedom in the Christian sense. When one regards God in purely categorial terms as one reality along with others, as one of the many objects of freedom of choice understood as a neutral capacity which occupies itself arbitrarily now with this and now with that, the statement that freedom of choice is freedom of choice even with respect to God offers no special difficulty. The extreme statement about the nature of freedom which, in its radicalness, leaves ordinary categorial indeterminism far behind, is that freedom is freedom even with regard to its supporting ground—that it can thus culpably deny the condition of its own possibility in an act which necessarily affirms this condition once again. What is decisive for the Christian doctrine of freedom is that this freedom involves the possibility of consent to or refusal of its own horizon, and that it is this possibility which properly constitutes freedom.

Of course human freedom, being freedom mediated in terms of the world, is always freedom as regards a categorial object, freedom as regards something in the world, even where it sets out to be immediately and explicitly freedom with respect to God. The reason for this is that even such an act as explicit consent to or refusal of God cannot be related immediately to the God of the basic transcendental experience, but only to the God of thematic categorial reflection—to God as a concept, not immediately and solely to the God of transcendental presence. But it is nevertheless part of the specifically Christian experience of freedom that this freedom is freedom not solely with respect to some object of categorial experience within the absolute context which is God, but that it is a freedom, if always only mediated, with respect to God Himself and turned toward Him: a freedom to accept or to reject God Himself. It follows, therefore, that it is not this alone or primarily where God is to be found and is conceived reflectively in categorial concepts, but where God is to be found prereflectively, but basically, in the transcendental experience which is a condition and constituent of every personal activity directed to our environment and our fellow men. In this sense we meet God in a most radical way everywhere, as the most authentic challenge to our freedom in everything in the world and—as the Bible says— above all in our neighbor.

To put the problem more exactly, one may ask why the transcendental context of freedom is not only the condition of its possibility but also its proper object. Or to put it another way, one wonders why it is not enough for us to act in freedom with respect to ourselves, our environment, and our fellow men. It is understood, of course, that the result of such free action, whether fulfilling or negating, lies always within that infinitely large horizon of transcendence from which we confront these objects of our free act. Finally, there is the question of why this horizon itself is also the *object* of this freedom, in the acceptance and rejection of it, when by definition this horizon remains the condition of the possibility of its own rejection. This condition inescapably requires that in this rejection the horizon is necessarily and inevitably affirmed as the condition of the possibility of freedom, and at the same time denied as unreflected-on object. Thus in this act of negating freedom we find the real and absolute contradiction in which God is simultaneously accepted and rejected. This ultimate enormity is at the same time reduced and relativized into the temporal, in the sense that it is necessarily objectified in and mediated through the finite substance of our life in its being spread through time.

We have to insist on the real possibility of such an absolute contradiction in freedom precisely because this possibility is the object of dispute and doubt. This happens in popular theology when people say that it is inconceivable that the infinite God in His objectivity can assess the tiny deformity of some finite reality, the offense against some particular, purely finite thing, except in terms of what it presently is: something *finite*. The argument runs that therefore God cannot evaluate it in terms of some absolute prohibition and infinite sanction, or describe it as directed against His own will as such. The "will" against which the offense is really directed in such a sin would be the God-willed finite thing, and an offense against God's will over and above this would be making God's will illegitimately into a particular categorial thing alongside the thing willed. Nevertheless, the possibility exists of a rejection, through freedom, with respect to God Himself. Otherwise real subjectivity in freedom would be impossible, for its specific quality is a matter of the subject, because it is transcendence.

If the particular things in the world which we meet within the horizon of transcendence are not occurrences in a space which remains unaffected by what it encloses but rather the materialization in history of the self-presentation and accessibility for encounter of this source of our transcendence which supports our subjectivity, then freedom with respect to the particular things we meet is also always freedom with respect to the horizon, the ground, the "abyss," which allows them to meet us and become the inner constituent of our receptive freedom. Inasmuch as the term and source cannot be a matter of indifference for the subject as knower, but are explicitly or implicitly what this cognitive transcendence has to do with even when it does not have this term as explicit object, the subject has the *freedom* to concern itself with God Himself, basically and inescapably, even when this freedom is always realized and mediated in the concrete particularity of experience.

Basically, freedom is freedom to accept or reject God, and is thus freedom of the subject in regard to Himself. If the subject as such is supported precisely by his transcendental immediacy to God, then truly subjective freedom, such as finally orders the subject as a whole, can take place only in accepting or rejecting God, because only there can the subject as such be met with at all. Otherwise, freedom would be some indifferent freedom to choose this or that; it would be an infinitely perpetuated repetition of the same or of the opposite (only a kind of the same); it would be a freedom of the eternal return of the same wandering Jew. The alternative must be the freedom of the subject in relation to himself in his definitive status, and hence freedom as regards God; however little this ground, this most proper and basic object of freedom may be reflected on in the particular act of freedom.

Another consideration brings to light the ultimate theological ground of freedom as freedom before God. If the grace-informed materialization in history of our transcendence is supported by the self-communication of God offered to us; if our transcendence as spirit is never to be found as something purely natural but is always embraced and supported by a grace-informed impulse of our being as spirit toward absolute nearness to God; if, in other words, God never becomes present only as the constantly elusive and retreating context of our transcendence but offers Himself as such for immediate possession in what we call divinizing grace—then freedom receives, in transcendence and in accepting or rejecting its ground, a certain immediacy to God through which it becomes in the most radical way the capacity to accept and reject God as such. This capacity is not found in the abstract, formal concept of transcendence to God as merely the remote and elusive context of our existence.

From the Christian point of view, as we said before, freedom cannot be regarded as a neutral capacity to do this or that in any order one prefers and in a condition of time which could be interrupted only from outside, although time could run on indeterminately so far as freedom is concerned. Freedom is rather the capacity to realize oneself once and for all, the capacity which of its nature involves the freely achieved, definitive status of the subject as such. This is obviously what is at issue in Christian language about man and his salvation or damnation, when he must answer, and be able to answer, as one who is free, for himself and for the whole of his life, before the judgment of God. The eternally valid verdict over his definitive salvation or damnation is passed, according to his works, by a judge who does not look upon the mere surface of life, on the "face," but who looks rather on the center of the person over whom he freely disposes, on the "heart." It is true that man's formal freedom to decide and choose is more taken for granted in Scripture than made the theme of conscious reflection. The explicit theme of Scripture, especially in the New Testament, is rather the paradox that the freedom of man, while remaining answerable and without being annulled, is nevertheless enslaved under the demonic powers of sin and death, and to some degree under the Law. It must be freed by the grace of God in an interior inclination for the Law. Thus it cannot be doubted that for Scripture the sinner and the justified man are answerable before God for the deed that sums up their life, and that they are also free to the extent that freedom is a permanent constituent of human nature.

But the authentic nature of this freedom, for Christian revelation, emerges only in so far as it is the basis for absolute salvation or damnation—really definitive and before God. In ordinary, everyday experience, freedom of choice may well look like a feature of some particular human act which can be imputed to a man to the extent that it had been actively performed by him, without this having been causally fixed in advance, and in this sense being forced by some interior condition of the man or by some outside situation which preceded the active decision. Such a concept of freedom of choice, however, atomizes freedom in exercise because it divides it up into nothing but someone's particular acts which are then held together only by some neutral substance—like identity of the subject who performs them all, and of his capacity to do so, and by the single exterior space time in which life is lived. Freedom would thus be nothing but freedom of *action*; it would be the possibility of imputing some particular act to a person who would remain neutral in himself and therefore always able to determine himself to something new, so long as the exterior conditions are given.

Yet from the Christian point of view man can determine and dispose over himself as a whole and for good and all through his freedom. Thus he does not perform acts which are to be qualified purely and morally and which then turn out to be entirely passing—acts which are charged to him only juridically or morally. On the contrary, by his free decision, at the heart of his being and in all truth, a man really *is* good or evil, and in such a way that his definitive salvation or damnation is already to be found in this decision, even if it is still hidden. The freedom in which one must answer for oneself is thus transformed and deepened in a terrifying fashion. Freedom is above all freedom of *being*. It is not only the quality of an act occasionally performed in fact or of the capacity to perform it. It is a transcendental "marking" of the human being itself. If man is really to be capable of disposing over himself for good and all, if eternity is thus to be the act of his own freedom, if this act is to be capable, in certain circumstances, of pulling something permanently good against its own goodness into a ruin which could make this man good or evil in the very ground of his being, and if this being good or evil is not something that hits a man from outside—then freedom must be regarded above all as freedom of being. That is to say, man is the being in whose being being itself is at issue. Man is that being which always has a relationship to itself—one of subjectivity, not simply of nature. Man is always a person; he is not simply "there" but is always *aware* of being there.

Nothing happens to this being in disregard of its relationship to itself; or if anything does so happen to it, then it is subjectively and savingly significant for it, to the extent that it is freely "understood," subjectively accepted, by a free subject as such in a wholly particular way. The "I" of this being cannot be overlooked or objectified. It can never be replaced or explained by another, not even by its own reflective conception of itself. It is pure source, not dependent on anything else, and therefore not capable of being derived from anything else or of being founded on anything else. Its relation to its divine source should not be interpreted in terms of causal and functional relations of dependence such as prevail in the realm of our categorial experience, in which the source retains and binds down instead of setting free, and in which being autonomous, and having a source, grow not in equal but in converse proportion. Through his freedom of being, man is always incomparable. He never fits adequately into any system; he can never be adequately subsumed by any idea. In a basic sense he is unassailable, yet at the same time he is alone and in danger. He is burdened with himself; he has no way of "absolving" himself from having to be himself, alone and once and for all; he has no way of shifting responsibility for himself on to somebody else.

In freedom, it is not a matter of choosing this or that, or of something which can be done or left undone. Basically, freedom is not the capacity to choose some object or to behave in some particular way with regard to this or that. It is the freedom of self-understanding, the possibility of saying yes or no to oneself, the possibility of decision for or against oneself. This possibility corresponds to the self-appropriation in knowledge, to the cognitional subjectivity, of man. Freedom never takes place as a purely objective process, as a mere choice "between" particular objects. On the contrary, it is the *self*-realization of the man who is choosing objectively, and it is only within this freedom in which man has power over himself that he is then also free with regard to the raw material of his self-realization. He can perform a certain act or abstain from it in regard to his own self-realization, something that is inescapably laid upon him. It is his inescapable task, and whatever the variation in the raw material of this self-realization, it is always a self-fulfillment directed toward God, or a radical self-refusal in face of God. For the salvation or damnation in the winning or losing God, something which is fixed in freedom, should not be regarded as a sheer external reaction of a judging or rewarding God. On the contrary, it is itself already achieved in this freedom.

Thus freedom is the capacity for something total. If it is to be able to bring about salvation or damnation, and thus to determine the whole man, it brings the whole man into play, in his past and in his future, in all the complexity of his self-world-God relationships. Freedom is always the self-realization of man choosing objectively in regard to a total realization, a total disposal over his existence in the sight of God. Thus it is easy to see that this basic feature of freedom is exercised in time. At any given moment the total project of existence to which we have referred, one's own total self-understanding, one's *option fondamentale*, remains empty in a multitude of ways, and objectively unrealized. The same actual depth and radicalness of self-disposal are not to be found in every individual act of freedom. All individual acts of freedom, although each of them means to engage in the venture of total and definitive self-disposal, are inserted into the whole of the one whole deed of freedom which recapitulates the one human, temporal, finite life. This is so precisely because each of these acts is performed within the context of the whole of existence and thereby receives its weight and proportion.

Accordingly, in the biblical and Augustinian concept of the heart, in the concept of subjectivity in Kierkegaard, in that of action in Blondel, and so on, there is always appreciation of the fact that there is this basic act of freedom, embracing and marking the whole existence. Of course this act is realized by means of man's particular acts, by means of acts which may be localized in space and time, and which may be objectified in their motives; it cannot be performed in any other way. But it cannot be simply identified in objective reflection with any such individual act. Neither does it represent the pure moral result of the sum of these individual acts, nor is it to be identified simply with the moral quality of the last of one's freely performed individual acts. The concrete freedom of man in which in the sight of God he disposes of himself as a whole in procuring his own definitive status in the sight of God is the unity in difference (no longer capable of being reflected on) of *option fondamentale* and of one's individual free acts, a unity which is the concrete being of the free subject who has realized himself. Thus, to insist upon the point once more, freedom is not the capacity of being always able to do the opposite, of infinite revision. It is the capacity to do something for good and all, the capacity to do something which is valid forever precisely because it is done in freedom. Freedom is the capacity for the eternal. Natural processes can always be revised again and altered; this is why they are indifferent. The result of freedom is the true necessity which remains forever.

Freedom is mystery because it derives from and is directed to God alone, and God is essentially the incomprehensible mystery which as such is precisely the source and term of freedom as such. The ground of freedom is the "abyss" of the mystery, which can never be regarded as something not yet known but which one day will be comprehensible. It is the most basic datum of our transcendental experience in knowledge and love. In its manifest and permanent incomprehensibility it is the ground of the possibility of comprehending everything which is encountered as an individual within its context.

We must forgo putting the epistemological question about how far freedom can really be known. Freedom is not a datum of any empirical psychology, because this discipline can do no more than observe functional connections between particular data within the context of experience, while freedom is always experienced before any such objective experience, as a modality of any transcendental experience. The subject freely knows himself *as not* objectifiable.

This radical mysteriousness of the freedom of the subject is thus inserted into the free act of this subject as such. The particular act of freedom shares in the mystery of his origin and future in so far as it is never absolutely objectifiable in its freedom and thus in its moral quality. Of course this peculiarity derives immediately from the strict subjectivity of freedom, but it is also insisted on explicitly in Revelation. It is to be found there that freedom and the concrete free decision are ultimately unobjectifiable. That total decision in which one disposes forever and ever over the whole of one's being and which fixes this wholeness itself in its freely determined definitive state—and only in so far as this happens can a particular act really be called fully free—is submitted, according to Revelation, to the sole judgment of God.

Man brings about his definitive status in freedom and therefore as a *conscious* subject, but he cannot objectify for himself this product of his freedom. That is to say, he cannot judge himself or anybody in his total quality in the sight of God. It is the Catholic doctrine of faith that *homo viator* is denied an absolutely certain judgment about his state of justification or his eternal salvation. The Protestant doctrine of justification—in spite of a tradition of controversy—does not disagree on this point, because even in the Lutheran doctrine of justification, faith regarded as absolute trust can still be tempted. This means that man cannot reflect his free decision with objective adequacy or with absolute certainty. Freedom is truly subjectivity, and subjectivity in itself and in its self-assimilation objectifies a more basic experience than the purely material, the present at hand, and the objective; and it can be unambiguously defined by a precedent and more basic system of coordinates made up of general concepts. In the act of his freedom man knows who he is in freedom and who he wants to be. But this very knowing is really nothing but himself, and therefore he cannot remove it from himself as something objective and manipulable and say as clearly to himself that he declares himself for God in his freedom. This declaration, which is himself, disappears from his sight, in a certain measure, into the mystery of God. An absolutely certain declaration about a man's exercise of freedom in a particular act which could be localized in space and time is fundamentally impossible for this man himself and all the more so for other people.

Of course this does not mean that freedom and responsibility are not things which are to be found in the realm of human experience and reflection and among human beings. Freedom, even in the form of concrete, total self-disposal of the free subject over himself for good and all, still takes place in some given particular categorial materials: subjectivity is always realized in nature. That shows the creatureliness of human freedom. It is equally clear that, without prejudice to the impossibility of any adequate self-reflection, man is always the one who reflects, the one who objectifies himself, the one who places himself under norms of general validity. It is Catholic teaching and—if one considers the morality present materially in the Bible—also thoroughly biblical teaching, that what is developed is more than purely formal principles of the subjective exercise of freedom of the subject with regard to its rightness or wrongness. Developed thoroughly also are material norms of an objective and generally valid kind with regard to right or wrong exercise of this subjective freedom in the categorial material of the nature of man and his world. This result makes it obvious that man is no less authorized than obliged to make a certain reflective and objectified self-judgment of his moral state and thus a judgment with regard to the givenness, rightness, or wrongness of his exercise of freedom in a particular material act.

This knowledge about oneself, which one can tell oneself, which one can examine critically, with regard to which one can arrive at some valid result, is characteristic precisely of the peculiar nature of the pilgrim existence of man in this life, in which freedom is still always at work, and in which every examination is itself still an act of freedom not adequately examined or examinable in a reflective way. It is real knowledge; it gives a "certainty"—the kind of certainty that can be found in the realm of history and freedom—that is to say, the demand to subject freedom itself, once more and necessarily, to norms. One has the right and the duty to include this knowledge of oneself—and eventually his knowledge about other people as well—in the calculus of one's life and one's active deciding and behaving, because otherwise one cannot exist at all. In any case, complete abstention from such a judgment does not escape the risk of such a judgment. On the contrary, it would be itself merely another free and risk-laden decision. Yet this knowledge of freedom, judging, deciding, venturing, and objectifying is not to be regarded as something definitive, absolutely certain, beyond appeal. In this objectified knowledge man accepts himself in his own reflective mode of self-understanding, which is itself just another act of unreflected freedom. Precisely as the one who understands himself in some way or another, man surrenders himself to the mysterious judgment of God, which takes place secretly in the unreflected act of his freedom. Freedom is mystery.

Man's freedom is, in fact, free self-realization into a definitive state. But despite its authentically creative character, it is nonetheless a created freedom. That this freedom is created is apparent for two reasons. This freedom is lived and experienced above all in its transcendental being as supported and empowered by its absolute context, something it does not constitute, but something by which it is constituted. The transcendentality of spirit should not be understood either in knowing or in the free act of living, in the sense that spirit projects and fixes its term and its goal. This goal discloses itself to the knowing and willing spirit in a particular mode of retreat—this is not ontologism. The goal is experienced in the act of spiritual existence itself in terms of the authentically moving cause. The active self-projection of spirit toward its goal, toward its future, is experienced as supported by the self-disclosing goal, over which the spirit does not dispose, because it does not comprehend this goal. On the contrary, in being and in operation it is constituted by it as that which lies beyond it. The specific nature of the transcendentality of freedom, as something supported and empowered by its goal, itself points to the createdness of this freedom, which is immediately experienced as posited.

The character of created freedom is strengthened and clarified by the empowering self-disclosure of this goal. This strengthening occurs because the empowering of freedom for the absoluteness of being is experienced as grace-informed empowering for absolute nearness to this goal in immediate self-communication of this goal—that is, divine grace—even if this experience can be clearly objectified only by its interpretation in supernatural revelation and faith. Grace as nearness to God radicalizes the experience of the createdness of freedom. There is further confirmation of the character of created freedom, as the subjects's self-disposal over himself for good and all, is necessarily mediated by an environment and a community which are given *a posteriori*, uncontrollably, ultimately unplanned. Man accomplishes his basic freedom toward himself always only in going acceptingly through the course of his own given history, something which is given in advance, something which is imposed as a task. Freedom is free to answer to necessity, in acceptance or rejection. Thus its createdness emerges once again.

Creaturely freedom is conditioned by a situation in the sense that it comes to itself only in so far as it goes out into the world. According to Christian doctrine, contained above all in the implications of the doctrine of original sin and of concupiscence, this state of being conditioned by a situation is distinguished by the fact that this situation is always and inescapably determined to some extent by guilt. In other words, the doctrine that there was sin at the beginning of man's history and the doctrine of concupiscence together mean that there is never a situation or any raw material of freedom for the freedom of man—if situation and raw material are seen adequately and without arbitrary abstractions—which would not be partly determined in advance by the guilt in the history of mankind to the particular positive or negative moral decision.

Further, it is never possible, before the end of history, to succeed wholly in eliminating this mortgage of guilt which is objectified in the situation. In so far as freedom must always objectify itself in some alien material, in order to find itself, it is always alienated from itself. It can never see itself so clearly in what it has done in the raw material of the situation in order to be itself that it can recognize in it exactly and with absolute certainty what it is: the acceptance or rejection of itself and of God. That is already clear from the fact that there is no objectification of which one could say with absolute certainty that it could arise in its concrete form out of freedom alone and not out of nature.

Since it is mediated in created terms, this freedom becomes unavoidably ambiguous, in an ultimate sense, in its objectification. Thus it becomes a mystery, and as such it must surrender itself to God. This ambiguity of the objectifications of freedom for its reflection on its basic nature is now made sharper by the circumstance that the material which is given in advance to freedom and which enters into its concrete exercise is always to some extent determined and shaped by the guilt from the beginning of the history of the spirit. Of course the freedom of the individual can always regard this material, which is partly determined by the guilt of others and which does not remain outside the act of freedom, in the sense that it ratifies the guilt-determinedness of this material as embodiment of its own refusal of God, in the sense that it makes it the objective manifestation of its own guilt. On the other hand, it may understand it in the sense that it suffers it and overcomes it in consent to God by participating in the cross of Christ. But this very ambiguity of the given situation and of its material for the exercise of freedom once again makes the basic act of freedom a mystery that is ultimately not absolutely open to reflection and not finally soluble—a mystery for freedom itself. It conceals the meaning and the quality of the history of mankind as a whole in the unsearchable judgment of God.

In so far as freedom is always, in every act, freedom for the mystery of God himself, the mystery by which it is supported and empowered, the act of freedom is always essentially the act of man's self-surrender to the uncontrollable disposal of God, and in this sense it is essentially a trustful risk. In the history of this freedom's self-experience it becomes evident only very gradually how God gives Himself to this freedom which, if it does not want to avoid Him, must trust itself to Him unconditionally in the venture of freedom into what cannot be controlled. This history of the experience of freedom—what we call the history of salvation and revelation—is the experience accomplished in Jesus Christ. God, in what we call divinizing grace, has given Himself into the possession of the freedom of man, in absolute nearness, and as basis of the free acceptance of this nearness. God in His inmost divinity has delivered Himself to the freedom which delivers itself into the uncontrollable mystery of God. God is not merely the remote context in which, as something always more removed, man projects his free self-understanding. On the contrary, God has become the realm and object of this exercise of freedom in absolute immediacy.

Thus it has become manifest in this experience of freedom that the rejection of God by man, which affects the whole of the history of human freedom, was allowed by God only in the divine consent to His own self-communication to creaturely freedom and that it remains embraced by this consent of God, which is what remains for everyone victorious in the whole history of salvation. The freedom of man is freed into immediacy to the freedom of being of God Himself. It is empowered to its highest possible act, the act which involves its formal nature but which is not demanded by it. The freedom which is directed toward God and derived from Him as origin and future of freedom, freedom as the capacity for dialogue possessed by love, is exercised in the highest conceivable modality of this aspect. It is freedom which is supported by God's self-communication in personal love and which embraces God Himself. The context and the object of love freely bestowed have become identical.